DAIRY-FREE
food for kids

DAIRY-FREE
food for kids

**More than 100 quick & easy recipes
for lactose-intolerant children**

Nicola Graimes

hamlyn

To Ella, Joel, and Silvio, with love.

An Hachette UK Company
www.hachette.co.uk

First published in Great Britain in 2015 by Hamlyn,
a division of Octopus Publishing Group Ltd
Carmelite House
50 Victoria Embankment
London EC4Y 0DZ
www.octopusbooks.co.uk
www.octopusbooksusa.com

Distributed in the US by Hachette Book Group,
1290 Avenue of the Americas, 4th and 5th Floors,
New York, NY 10020

Distributed in Canada by Canadian Manda Group,
664 Annette St., Toronto, Ontario, Canada M6S 2C8

Nicola Graimes asserts the moral right to be identified as the author of this work.

ISBN 978-0-600-63217-7

Printed and bound in China.

10 9 8 7 6 5 4 3 2 1

Standard level kitchen spoon and cup measurements are used in all recipes.

Ovens should be preheated to the specified temperature; if using a convection oven,
follow the manufacturer's instructions for adjusting the time and temperature.

Fresh herbs should be used unless otherwise stated.

Large eggs should be used unless otherwise stated.

The U.S. Food and Drug Administration advises that eggs should not be consumed
raw. This book contains some dishes made with raw or lightly cooked eggs.
It is prudent for vulnerable people, such as pregnant and nursing mothers,
people with weakened immune systems, the elderly, babies, and young children,
to avoid uncooked or lightly cooked dishes made with eggs. Once prepared,
these dishes should be kept refrigerated and used promptly.

This book includes dishes made with nuts and nut derivatives. It is advisable for those
with known allergic reactions to nuts and nut derivatives and those who may be
potentially vulnerable to these allergies to avoid dishes made with nuts and nut oils.
It is also prudent to check the labels of prepared ingredients for the possible inclusion
of nut derivatives.

contents

introduction

Introducing kids to healthy eating habits and a positive attitude to food is a really important part of parenting. From initial weaning and moving to solids, to overcoming food fads, food aversions, and enjoying a varied and balanced diet, eating habits that are formed during childhood can last a lifetime. However, when you have to work around a food allergy or intolerance, it can take a lot more planning and perseverance to lay the groundwork for a healthy approach to—and enjoyment of—food.

Mealtimes have to be thought through in advance and social occasions require careful planning. You will also need to consider the balance between giving your child all the information he or she needs to manage an allergy or intolerance and not allowing it to become a burden or impact upon his or her everyday life more than is absolutely necessary.

We are more aware of milk allergy and lactose intolerance these days—symptoms are generally noticed early on and a timely diagnosis of the conditions means that your child won't suffer unnecessarily. You can then introduce alternatives and substitutes that will make sure of a well-balanced diet and healthy development.

Allergy or intolerance?

Despite better diagnosis and a greater understanding of food allergies and intolerances, many people still confuse the two and are unsure of the different causes, symptoms, and management of each condition. In order to make it easier to differentiate between the two, modern medicine classifies a food allergy as an immune-related condition and a food intolerance as a nonimmune-related condition.

This basically means that if your child has a milk allergy, his or her immune system is unable to cope with milk protein and will reject it. Reactions can range from severe diarrhea, skin complaints, and facial swelling to dizziness or anaphylactic shock (although this is a rare reaction). People with a milk allergy will have a reaction if they consume even a tiny amount of milk proten, which means dairy produce must be completely avoided.

Lactose intolerance is a slightly more forgiving condition in that people who have it may still be able to consume lactose in small quantities and the condition can be managed. We digest lactose (the sugar in milk) with an enzyme called lactase, which breaks down lactose so it can be easily absorbed by the body. Children with lactose intolerance don't produce enough lactase, which means the lactose stays in the digestive system and ferments. As with any fermentation process, this produces gas, which is why the symptoms of lactose intolerance include bloating, stomachaches, diarrhea, and gas.

Dairy-free diagnosis

Diagnosing a milk allergy

Most children with a milk allergy develop symptoms soon after drinking milk or eating dairy produce. This means you will probably link the symptoms to dairy consumption early on and you should see your physician as soon as you have any concerns. A scratch test in which the skin is pricked to let an allergen into the skin is the usual way of diagnosing a milk allergy and results are available within minutes. Blood tests may be needed to check for an allergy and you'll have to wait for definitive results. In the meantime, you might be advised to remove dairy from your child's diet and use substitutes. Once a positive diagnosis has been returned, you'll need to see a dietitian to discuss your options for alternatives to dairy, and to be sure your child gets all his or her nutritional requirements from other food sources.

Diagnosing lactose intolerance

Lactose intolerance can be harder to diagnose, because it is a digestive condition. Kids are mini germ factories; they pick up endless stomach complaint,s and flus seem to be on constant rotation around nurseries and schools. However, you might start to notice that your child complains of stomachache an hour or two after drinking milk or eating diary. If you have your suspicions, make a note of what your child has eaten on the days he or she complains of cramps or pains, or has any other symptoms. Make an appointment with your physician to discuss your concerns; it will probably be recommended that your child avoids dairy for a week or two to see if the symptoms ease.

Some of the tests for diagnosing lactose tolerance are not suitable for infants and young children because the symtpoms can be severe. Instead, a stool acidity test can be taken after the child drinks a small quantity of milk. However, more simply, if symptoms disappear once lactose is removed from the diet, you can be pretty certain that your child is lactose intolerant.

Growing out of allergies

If your child is diagnosed with a milk allergy, you should not assume that this is a life-long condition. The majority of children grow out of milk allergies by the age of four or five. This means it is important to get your child tested regularly—it can be done every six months or so. That way, you can readjust your child's diet once he or she has outgrown the condition, and reintroduce dairy. Lactose intolerance, however, is something your child may have to live with throughout life. If your body doesn't begin to produce enough lactase when you are younger, it is unlikely to suddenly start producing it later on in life. Many people actually develop lactose intolerance during adulthood, as the body can diminish its production of lactase with age.

Introducing a dairy-free diet

Once your child has been diagnosed with a milk allergy or lactose intolerance, you will need to make some fundamental changes to his or her diet. This basically means avoiding all milk drinks and dairy products and replacing these with foods and drinks that will match the nutritional value of dairy. Below is a list of the main dairy foods that should be avoided:

- Milk (including nonfat dry milk powder)
- Butter
- Buttermilk

- Cream
- Cheese (including cream cheese)
- Quark
- Ice cream
- Ghee
- Curd
- Yogurt
- Puddings

Check the label

It will be fairly easy to avoid the main culprits, but if your child has a serious reaction to dairy, it is vital to check food labels. Dairy products can hide in all kinds of foods, including cereal, bread products, cakes, cookies, soups, chocolate bars, TV dinners, and sauces. It might not be obvious that the food contains a milk product, so you'll need to look for dairy-linked ingredients, such as casein, hydrolysates, lactalbumin, lactalbumin phosphate, lactose, lactoglobulin, lactoferrin, lactulose, rennet, whey, and whey products. You will eventually get to grips with what's lurking deep down in the ingredients list of every container and package you add to your shopping cart but, for now, it's a case of carefully checking every label.

Dairy alternatives

So, now that you know the foods to avoid, you'll need to stock up on some alternatives to be sure your child still enjoys a full and varied diet and doesn't miss his or her favorite meals and snacks. Milk is the obvious starting point and it's worth checking if your child is intolerant to all milk, or just cow milk. If not, sheep, goat and buffalo milk make good alternatives.

If you must avoid all animal milk, soy milk will be top of your shopping list. It is extremely versatile and is available in sweetened and unsweetened varieties and different flavors. Soy also takes care of dairy-free yogurt, cream, and cheese dilemmas and again, these come in different flavors and varieties. Almond, rice, oat, and coconut milk are also worth trying.

The health factor

When cutting out a food group from children's diets, it's important to be sure they are getting enough vitamins and minerals from other sources. When we think of dairy products, calcium is the first mineral that springs to mind. Essential for bone development and muscle movement, kids also need to keep up their calcium levels in order to avoid medical conditions, such as osteoporosis, later on in life.

Although it's true that dairy products are a major source of calcium, there are many foods that will help kids to get their recommended 1,000 mg a day (children over nine years need 1,300 mg a day). These are some good sources:

- Tofu
- Almonds
- Sesame seeds
- Tahini
- Collard greens
- Soybeans (edamame)
- Molasses
- Hazelnuts
- Watercress
- Chickpeas
- Figs
- Parsley
- Leafy green vegetables.

more confident about the food choices they make. And by showing your child just how delicious a dairy-free diet can be with good homecooked food, they won't feel like they are missing anything.

Don't limit your lifestyle

Any dietary conditions that are imposed instead of chosen can be a burden on those who have to follow them. This is especially true for children—at the time in their lives when they should be exploring new ingredients and flavors, their diet is suddenly limited, with painful consequences if they step outside the boundaries. However, this also provides opportunities to seek out exciting ingredients that your family might not have tried if it were not for a milk allergy or dairy intolerance. It will encourage you to become more adventurous and creative in the kitchen, and your kids will be better informed about their health and well-being.

Keep your kids informed

Although it may be important that you know the scientific names of every milk product that could potentially make its way into your pantry, it's equally important that your child is aware of the foods that he or she should avoid. When children are especially young, you have complete control over their diet. However, as soon as they start nursery or school, or get asked to friends' houses, they need an understanding of their condition and to be aware of the foods they can't eat.

Of course, you can talk to the school and other parents to let them know which foods your child should avoid, but it's unrealistic to assume that everyone will remember all of the time. If your child is aware of the foods he or she can't eat from an early age, he or she will be more knowledgeable and confident about telling people about having a milk allergy or lactose intolerance when away from home. Make sure adults at play dates, parties, and outings have your contact details so they can quickly and easily contact you if your child becomes ill.

The recipes in this book will make life easier, and if you cook them with your child, they will learn more about the ingredients they can and can't eat and will become

About the book

The recipes in this book demonstrate that dairy-free food is exciting, varied, and full of flavor. Instead of focusing on the ingredients you have to remove from your child's diet, we celebrate all the incredible ingredients that can be included. There's a selection of snacks, such as Cheesy Popcorn, Crispy Chickpea Bites, and Spicy Squash Hummus; quick and easy weekday meals, including Chicken Cashew Curry and Salmon and Potato Tortilla; and special dinner ideas for the weekend, everything from Smoked Salmon and Kale Risotto to Thai Tofu Burgers and Sweet and Sour Pork Balls. A selection of desserts and treats makes sure sweet teeth are catered for, and kids will clamor for Peanut Butter and Choc Chip Cookies, Fruity Ice Pops, Banana Melts, and Chocolate Beet Brownies.

Although these recipes have been created with dairy-free diets in mind, they can be enjoyed by the whole family—there's no need to prepare different meals simply because your child has a milk allergy or dairy intolerance. From family gatherings to kids' sleepovers, Saturday movie nights to lazy Sunday brunches, these recipes will get kids excited about mealtimes by digging into nutritious food that doesn't need dairy products to make it work.

breakfast

pancakes with apple butter

Serves 4

Preparation time 15 minutes,
  plus standing

Cooking time 35–40 minutes

1⅔ cups all-purpose flour

1½ teaspoons baking powder

pinch of salt

2 tablespoons superfine or
  granulated sugar

1¼ cups unsweetened dairy-free milk

2 eggs, lightly beaten

sunflower oil or dairy-free spread,
  for frying

Apple butter

4 crisp, sweet apples, peeled, cored,
  and chopped

¼ cup water

1 cinnamon stick

½–1 teaspoon allspice, to taste

To serve

maple syrup or honey

dairy-free yogurt

This quick version of traditional apple butter, which is basically a concentrated fruit spread, is a great alternative to sugary preserves. The spices are naturally sweet, so you don't need to add extra sugar to the fruit.

1 Sift the flour, baking powder, and salt into a large bowl, then stir in the sugar and make a well in the center. Whisk together the milk and eggs in a small bowl, then pour into the dry ingredients and stir to make a smooth batter. Let stand for 20 minutes.

2 Meanwhile, make the apple butter. Put the apples into a saucepan with the measured water and cinnamon stick, cover, and cook over low heat for 20 minutes, stirring frequently and adding a splash more water, if necessary, until the apples are soft and mushy. Remove the cinnamon stick, stir in the allspice to taste, then mash with the back of a fork until smooth. Spoon the apple mixture into a ramekin and set aside.

3 Heat a little oil or spread in a large nonstick skillet over medium heat, add 3 tablespoons of the batter for each pancake, and cook for 2 minutes on each side, until light golden. Remove from the pan and keep warm in a low oven. Repeat with the remaining batter to make about 16 pancakes, adding more oil or spread to the pan as necessary.

4 Top the cakes with the apple butter and a drizzle of maple syrup or honey and serve with yogurt.

banana yogurt crunch

Serves 2

Preparation time 10 minutes, plus cooling

Cooking time 5–6 minutes

⅓ cup rolled oats

2 tablespoons mixed seeds, such as
   sunflower, pumpkin, and sesame

4 teaspoons maple syrup or honey

1 cup dairy-free yogurt, preferably
   unsweetened

2 small bananas, sliced

1 Put the oats into a large, dry skillet and toast over medium-low heat for 3 minutes, stirring occasionally. Add the seeds and cook, stirring, for another 2–3 minutes, until golden.

2 Remove the pan from the heat and stir in the syrup or honey. It will sizzle at first, but keep stirring until the oats and seeds are evenly coated. Let cool until crisp.

3 Divide half of the oat mixture between 2 glasses, then top with half of the yogurt and bananas. Repeat with another layer of the remaining oat mixture, yogurt, and bananas.

pineapple & coconut shake

Serves 2

Preparation time 10 minutes

2 cups chopped fresh or canned pineapple (drained, if necessary)

1 cup coconut drinking milk (*see* page 135 for homemade)

⅓ cup coconut yogurt

1 teaspoon vanilla extract

½ teaspoon finely grated nutmeg

1 Put the pineapple, coconut milk, yogurt, vanilla extract, and three-quarters of the nutmeg into a blender and blend until smooth and creamy.

2 Pour into 2 glasses and sprinkle with the remaining nutmeg.

Hints and tips
If you can't find coconut yogurt, any dairy-free yogurt would be delicious in this breakfast shake.

spiced hot almond milk

Serves 1

Preparation time 5 minutes, plus steeping

Cooking time 5 minutes

1¼ cups unsweetened almond milk or other nut milk (*see* page 134 for homemade)

½ cinnamon stick

2 cloves

½ teaspoon vanilla extract

maple syrup, honey, or light brown sugar, to taste

To serve (optional)

ice cubes

freshly grated nutmeg

This version of the popular Spanish drink *horchata* is made with nut milk and flavored with spices. It makes a comforting, warming drink for any time of the day, but can also be served cold over ice.

1 Pour the milk into a small saucepan, add the cinnamon and cloves, and heat gently to almost boiling point, then turn off the heat and let steep for at least 15 minutes, or overnight in the refrigerator.

2 Remove the spices, then stir in the vanilla extract and syrup, honey, or sugar to taste. Reheat if serving warm, or serve cold or chilled over ice. Sprinkle with a little nutmeg, if desired.

mixed-grain coconut porridge

Serves 2

Preparation time 5 minutes

Cooking time 7–10 minutes

½ cup rolled oats

½ cup quinoa, millet, or buckwheat flakes

1¼ cups coconut drinking milk
  (*see* page 135), plus extra to serve

1¾ cups water

1 teaspoon ground cinnamon

1 ripe banana, mashed

1 tablespoon flaked unsweetened
  dried coconut, toasted

There are many different types of grain now available and it's worth trying all of them, because they are often supernutritious.

1 Put the oats and quinoa, millet, or buckwheat flakes into a medium saucepan. Pour in the milk and measured water, then stir in three-quarters of the cinnamon. Bring to a boil, reduce the heat to low, and simmer, partly covered, for 5–8 minutes, stirring frequently, until the grains are tender.

2 Spoon into 2 bowls and top with banana and coconut. Sprinkle with the remaining cinnamon and add extra milk to serve.

blueberry bircher muesli

Serves 2–3

**Preparation time 10 minutes,
  plus overnight soaking**

1 cup rolled oats

2 cups unsweetened almond milk
  (*see* page 134), plus extra to serve

3 tablespoons coconut yogurt

1 small crisp, sweet apple, cored and grated

2 teaspoons ground flaxseeds (optional)

maple syrup or honey, to taste (optional)

1 tablespoon sunflower seeds, toasted

handful of blueberries

allspice, to serve (optional)

This breakfast requires a little preplanning, because the oats need soaking overnight.

1 Put the oats into a bowl and pour the milk over them. Stir to combine, then cover and let soak in the refrigerator overnight.

2 Stir in the yogurt, apple, flaxseeds, if using, and a little syrup or honey to taste, if desired.

3 Spoon into bowls and add a splash of milk if too dry, then top with the sunflower seeds and blueberries. Serve sprinkled with allspice, if desired.

smoked salmon omelet

Serves 2

Preparation time 10 minutes

Cooking time 5 minutes

1 tablespoon dairy-free cream cheese

1 tablespoon dairy-free cream

1 teaspoon lemon juice

½ teaspoon finely grated lemon zest

1 tablespoon dairy-free spread

3 eggs, lightly beaten

4 oz smoked salmon pieces or 1 smoked mackerel fillet, skinned and flaked into small pieces

black pepper

This is a simplified, dairy-free version of an omelet that is topped with smoked salmon or mackerel and a cream cheese sauce.

1 Mix together the cream cheese, cream, and lemon juice and zest in a bowl and set aside.

2 Heat the spread in a medium, ovenproof skillet, then pour in the eggs. Turn the pan until the eggs coat the bottom in an even layer. When the bottom of the omelet is set but the top is still slightly runny, arrange the smoked salmon or mackerel on top, then add the cream cheese mixture in small spoonfuls.

3 Place the pan under a preheated medium-high broiler and cook for 2 minutes or until just cooked through. Season with black pepper, divide into 2, and serve.

breakfast muffin tortillas

Makes 8

Preparation time 10 minutes

Cooking time 15 minutes

olive oil, for greasing

8 eggs, lightly beaten

3 tablespoons nutritional yeast flakes

2 scallions, finely chopped

1 cooked, peeled red-skinned potato, cut into large cubes

3 cooked herb pork or vegetarian sausage links, cubed

4 cherry tomatoes, halved

salt and black pepper

For convenience, these individual breakfast tortillas are baked in a muffin pan, and they make a handy snack or light lunch.

1 Lightly grease 8 cups of a 12-cup muffin pan with oil.

2 Beat the eggs in a large bowl, stir in the yeast flakes, scallions, potato, and sausages, then season with salt and black pepper.

3 Spoon the mixture evenly into the prepared muffin pan, then place a tomato half on top of each tortilla. Place in a preheated oven, at 350°F, for 15 minutes or until the tortillas are cooked through. Let cool in the pan slightly, then turn out and serve.

Hints and tips
Feel free to adapt the fillings to your preferences: ham, spinach, corn kernels, peas, and shrimp all make good options.

potato cakes with smoked tofu

Serves 4

Preparation time 20 minutes

Cooking time 25–30 minutes

6 russet potatoes (about 1½ lb), cooked, cooled, and peeled

3 tablespoons dairy-free spread, melted

⅓ cup all-purpose flour, plus extra for dusting

½ egg, lightly beaten

2 tablespoons olive oil, plus extra for frying

8 oz smoked tofu, patted dry and cut into ½ inch cubes

4 large tomatoes, seeded and quartered

salt and black pepper

sweet chili sauce, to serve (optional)

A perfect way to use up leftover cooked potatoes, these cakes make a great weekend breakfast-cum-brunch. You also can't beat beans and a poached egg as an alternative to the smoked tofu topping.

1 Grate the cooked potatoes into a large bowl and stir in the spread, flour, and beaten egg. Season with salt and black pepper, then mix together until combined.

2 Transfer the potato mixture to a floured work surface. Dust the top with more flour and flatten to about ¾ inch thick. Stamp out 8 round cakes using a 2 inch plain pastry cutter.

3 Heat enough oil to coat the bottom of a large skillet over medium heat, add the potato cakes, and cook, in 2 batches, for 4–5 minutes on each side, until golden and cooked through. Reduce the heat slightly if they start to brown too quickly. Remove from the pan and drain on paper towels. Keep warm in a low oven while you cook the remaining potato cakes, adding more oil to the pan, if necessary.

4 Wipe the pan clean and heat 1 tablespoon of the oil over medium heat. Add the tofu and cook for 5–8 minutes, turning occasionally, until crisp all over. Remove from the pan and keep warm in the oven while you cook the tomatoes.

5 Heat the remaining oil in the pan, add the tomatoes, and cook for 2 minutes, until warmed through and starting to soften.

6 Serve the potato cakes topped with the tofu and tomatoes, drizzled with sweet chili sauce, if desired.

cheesy puff toasts

Serves 1–2

Preparation time 10 minutes

Cooking time 5 minutes

2 slices of whole-grain bread

1 egg, separated

1 teaspoon whole-grain mustard

2 tablespoons shredded dairy-free cheddar cheese alternative

1 tablespoon nutritional yeast flakes

To serve (optional)

broiled tomatoes

arugula

This soufflé topping for toast is as light as a cloud and easy to make.

1 Toast 1 side of each slice of bread under a preheated medium-high broiler. Meanwhile, mix together the egg yolk, mustard, cheese, and yeast flakes in a bowl. In a separate grease-free bowl, whisk the egg white until it forms stiff peaks. Gently fold the egg yolk mixture into the egg white.

2 Remove the toast from the broiler and place, toasted side down, on a plate. Spoon the cheese mixture over each slice of bread, then transfer to the broiler and cook for another 2 minutes or until the tops are puffy and golden.

3 Serve the toasts with broiled tomatoes and arugula, if desired.

mexican scrambled eggs

Serves 2

Preparation time 10 minutes

Cooking time 5 minutes

3 tablespoons dairy-free spread

3 scallions, finely chopped

½ red bell pepper, cored, seeded, and chopped

4 eggs

2 tablespoons unsweetened dairy-free milk

½ teaspoon Mexican spice blend

6 cherry tomatoes, quartered

4 corn taco shells

salt and black pepper

To serve (optional)

1 tablespoon chopped fresh cilantro

1 small avocado, pitted, peeled, and cubed

This breakfast-cum-brunch is a Mexican twist on the classic scrambled egg. Spooned into corn taco shells, the eggs are flavored with scallions, red bell pepper, and spices. Soft flour tortillas or even toast make good alternatives to the tacos, if you prefer.

1 Heat the spread in a skillet over medium heat, add the scallions and red bell pepper, and sauté for 2 minutes.

2 Mix together the eggs, milk, and spice blend in a bowl and season with salt and black pepper to taste.

3 Pour the egg mixture into the pan, reduce the heat to medium-low, and cook gently, stirring and folding the egg until scrambled. Just before the eggs are cooked, stir in the tomatoes to warm through.

4 Meanwhile, stand the taco shells on a baking sheet and place in a preheated oven, at 350°F, for 2–3 minutes, until warmed through.

5 Spoon the scrambled egg mixture into the taco shells. Sprinkle the cilantro and avocado over the top, if using, and serve.

snacks

crispy chickpea bites

Serves 4

Preparation time 5 minutes

Cooking time 35–45 minutes

1 (15 oz) can chickpeas, rinsed and drained

1 tablespoon olive oil or melted coconut oil

2 teaspoons Cajun spice mix or other spice blend

salt

1 Line a plate with paper towels, pour the chickpeas on top, and pat dry with a second sheet of paper towel.

2 Transfer the chickpeas to a bowl and stir in the oil, spice mix, and a large pinch of salt until thoroughly combined and evenly coated.

3 Spread the chickpeas on a baking sheet and place in a preheated oven, at 350°F, for 35–45 minutes, turning occasionally, until crisp and golden. Let cool before serving in paper cones. Store in an airtight container for up to 1 week.

seasoned popcorn

Serves 4

Preparation time 5 minutes

Cooking time 8 minutes

1½ tablespoons sunflower oil

100 g (3½ oz) popping corn

1 tablespoon nutritional yeast flakes

2 teaspoons smoked paprika or
  dried chives

A useful standby when a snack is called for!

1 Heat the oil in a large saucepan with a tight-fitting lid. Add the corn, cover, and heat until it starts to pop. Shake the pan occasionally and continue to cook until the popping stops.

2 Once all the kernels have popped, transfer the popcorn to a large bowl, add the yeast flakes and paprika or chives, and turn until the popcorn is coated in the flavorings. Serve immediately.

honey-soy nuts & seeds

Serves 4

Preparation time 5 minutes

Cooking time 8–10 minutes

2 cups unsalted nuts and seeds, such as almonds, cashew nuts, pistachios, hazelnuts, sunflower seeds, and pumpkin seeds (nuts and seeds kept separate)

1 tablespoon reduced-sodium soy sauce

1 teaspoon honey

A handful of nuts and seeds make a nutritious snack. These are flavored with a delicious combination of honey and soy sauce.

1 Place the nuts on a baking sheet and roast in a preheated oven, at 325°F, for 6 minutes.

2 Add the seeds to the sheet and turn until combined, then roast for another 2–4 minutes, until they smell toasted and start to brown. (Keep an eye on them, because they can burn easily.)

3 Transfer the nuts and seeds to a bowl, spoon the soy sauce and honey over them, and turn with a spoon until well coated. Let cool before serving. Store in an airtight container for up to 1 week.

cheesy tomato toasts

Serves 2

Preparation time 10 minutes

Cooking time 10 minutes

2 slices of seeded whole-grain bread

1 egg yolk

1 teaspoon Dijon mustard

few drops of Worcestershire sauce

1 tablespoon dairy-free cream cheese

1 teaspoon nutritional yeast flakes

1 tablespoon dairy-free spread

1 tablespoon all-purpose flour

¼ cup unsweetened dairy-free milk

4 cherry tomatoes, each cut into 6

carrot and celery sticks, to serve
(optional)

Fans of regular cheese on toast won't be disappointed with this dairy-free alternative.

1 Toast 1 side of each slice of bread under a preheated hot broiler. Transfer to a board, toasted side down. Meanwhile, beat together the egg yolk, mustard, Worcestershire sauce, cream cheese, and yeast flakes in a bowl, then set aside.

2 Melt the spread in a small saucepan, then whisk in the flour and cook over low heat for 1 minute, until it forms a light golden paste. Add the egg yolk mixture and heat through briefly, whisking continuously. Remove the pan from the heat, then stir in the milk. Return to low heat and cook for a few minutes, stirring continuously, until it forms a smooth, thick sauce.

3 Spoon the mixture over each slice of bread. Arrange the tomatoes on top, and broil for 2–3 minutes, until the tomatoes start to brown. Serve with carrot and celery sticks, if desired.

satay dip with pita chips

Serves 4–6

Preparation time 10 minutes

Cooking time 20 minutes

Satay dip

¼ cup peanut butter

1 garlic clove, crushed

1 tablespoon reduced-sodium soy sauce

1 tablespoon hoisin sauce

1 tablespoon sesame oil

1 teaspoon packed light brown sugar
or honey

¼ teaspoon dried red pepper flakes
(optional)

juice of ½ lime

¼ cup coconut drinking milk
(*see* page 135 for homemade)

½ cup water

Pita chips

4 pita breads

olive oil, for brushing

Perfect for dunking fresh vegetables or slices of crisp pita bread into, this Asian peanut dip can also be used as a sauce for noodles or rice.

1 Make the pita chips. Slice down the sides of each pita bread to open them out, then lightly brush both sides with olive oil. Place 1 pita in a large, dry skillet and toast for about 5 minutes, turning once, until crisp and golden. Remove from the pan and let cool. Repeat with the remaining pita breads.

2 Meanwhile, put all the dip ingredients into a small saucepan and heat gently, stirring, until warmed through and thickened.

3 Break the pita breads into large pieces and serve with the satay dip.

easy mushroom spread

Serves 4–6

Preparation time 15 minutes, plus soaking

Cooking time 20 minutes

½ oz dried porcini mushrooms

3 tablespoons dairy-free spread

1 tablespoon olive oil

1 onion, finely chopped

4 cups finely chopped cremini mushrooms

½ teaspoon dried thyme

2 garlic cloves, finely chopped

3 tablespoons dairy-free cream cheese

salt and black pepper

toast, pita bread, or crackers, to serve

1 Put the porcini into a heatproof bowl, cover with just-boiled water, and let soak for 20 minutes, until softened. Drain the mushrooms, reserving the soaking liquid, and finely chop.

2 Meanwhile, heat the spread and oil in a large skillet over medium heat, add the onion, and cook for 8 minutes, stirring frequently, until softened. Add the soaked porcini, cremini mushrooms, and thyme and cook for another 10 minutes, until soft and any liquid from the mushrooms has evaporated. Stir in the garlic, then let cool slightly.

3 Put the mushroom mixture into a food processor or blender with the cream cheese, season, and blend until smooth.

4 Spoon the mixture into a bowl and serve immediately, spread over toast, pita bread, or crackers. Alternatively, cover and store in the refrigerator for up to 5 days.

smoked salmon pâté

Serves 4

Preparation time 10 minutes

4 oz smoked salmon pieces

½ cup dairy-free cream cheese

2 tablespoons soy cream, plus extra if needed

juice of ½ lemon

1 tablespoon snipped chives

black pepper

toast, pita breads, or crackers, to serve

The creamy texture of this pâté makes it ideal for kids that are wary of fishy dishes.

1 Put the smoked salmon, cream cheese, cream, lemon juice, and chives into a food processor or blender. Season with black pepper and blend to an almost smooth pâté, adding a little extra cream, if necessary.

2 Spoon the pâté into a bowl and serve with strips of toast, pita breads, or crackers.

tuna cucumber cups

Serves 2

Preparation time 10 minutes

1 (5 oz) can tuna in spring water, drained
1 teaspoon reduced-sodium soy sauce
½ teaspoon sesame oil
1 scallion, finely chopped
6 inch piece of cucumber
2 teaspoons sesame seeds, toasted

Thick, round slices of cucumber make the perfect "cup," ready to be filled, once you scoop out the middle of the slices.

1 Mix together the tuna, soy sauce, sesame oil, and scallion in a bowl.

2 Cut the cucumber into 1 inch thick slices. Using a teaspoon, scoop the seeds out of each slice to form cup shapes, but leave the bottom intact.

3 Spoon the tuna mixture into the cups and sprinkle with sesame seeds before serving.

Hints and tips

In this recipe, the cucumber is stuffed with an Asian tuna mix, but the popular combination of tuna, corn kernels, scallion, and mayonnaise would also work well.

spicy squash hummus

Serves 4–6

Preparation time 15 minutes

Cooking time 30 minutes

½ butternut squash, peeled, seeded and cut into bite-size chunks

2 tablespoons extra virgin olive oil, plus extra to serve

1 teaspoon ground allspice (optional)

⅓ cup dairy-free yogurt, preferably unsweetened

2 tablespoons light tahini

1 garlic clove, crushed

juice of 1 lemon

1 teaspoon sesame seeds, toasted

salt and black pepper

Tahini is a calcium-rich sesame seed paste and makes a great addition to a dairy-free diet. It adds a slightly nutty flavor and creamy texture to soups, stews, dips, and sauces as well as this delicious hummus.

1 Put the squash, half the olive oil, and the allspice, if using, into a bowl and toss until the squash is well coated, then transfer to a baking sheet. Place in a preheated oven, at 375°F, for 30 minutes, turning once, until tender and starting to brown in places. Let cool for 5 minutes.

2 Transfer the squash to a food processor or blender, add the yogurt, tahini, garlic, lemon juice, and the remaining olive oil. Season, then blend until smooth. Alternatively, put the squash and other ingredients into a bowl and mash with a potato masher or the back of a fork. Add a little warm water if the mixture is too thick.

3 Spoon the hummus into a serving bowl, sprinkle with the sesame seeds, and drizzle with a little extra oil before serving.

coated cashew balls

Serves 4

**Preparation time 20 minutes,
  plus soaking**

1⅓ cups cashew nuts

½ cup cold water

1 garlic clove, crushed

2 teaspoons lemon juice

⅓ cup shelled unsalted pistachio nuts or
  other nuts or seeds, coarsely ground

⅓ cup finely chopped mixed herbs, such
  as oregano, chives, and parsley

salt and black pepper

toast, rice cakes, or crackers, to serve

1 Put the cashew nuts into a heatproof bowl, cover with hot water, and soak for at least 2 hours or overnight.

2 Drain the nuts, discarding the soaking water. Put into a food processor or blender, add the measured water, and blend to a coarse paste, scraping down the sides of the small bowl, if necessary. Transfer to a bowl, season with salt and black pepper, and stir in the garlic and lemon juice.

3 Put the ground pistachios and mixed herbs on separate plates. Shape 1 tablespoon of the cashew paste into a ball, then roll in the pistachios until evenly coated. Form a second ball, then roll it in the herbs. Repeat with the remaining cashew paste, rolling half of the balls in the nuts and half in the herbs. Transfer the coated balls to a plate, cover, and chill until slightly firm. Serve with toast, rice cakes, or crackers.

quesadillas

Serves 2

Preparation time 8 minutes

Cooking time 9–10 minutes

2 bacon slices

2 tablespoons dairy-free cream cheese

2 large white or seeded tortillas

¼ red onion, thinly sliced

1 tomato, sliced

handful of arugula or watercress leaves

olive oil, for frying

Filled with a delicious combination of bacon, red onion, tomato, and dairy-free cream cheese, this tortilla "sandwich" makes a quick, tasty snack. Let it stand for a couple of minutes after cooking until the filling has cooled and is slightly firm, otherwise it's in danger of running out when you cut into it.

1 Cook the bacon over an aluminum foil-lined broiler pan under a preheated hot broiler until cooked, turning once, then drain on paper towels. Cut into pieces and let one side.

2 Spread 1 tablespoon of the cream cheese over each tortilla. Arrange the onion, tomato, bacon, and arugula or watercress over 1 tortilla, then top with the remaining tortilla, cream cheese side down.

3 Drizzle a little oil over the bottom of a large skillet and heat over medium heat. Place the quesadilla in the pan, press the edges down slightly so the filling doesn't escape, and cook for 2–3 minutes or until golden and starting to crisp. Carefully turn the quesadilla over, using a spatula, and cook for another 2 minutes, until golden.

4 Slide the quesadilla out of the pan onto a serving plate and let cool for a few minutes. Cut into wedges to serve with arugula or watercress leaves.

socca pizza

Serves 6–8

Preparation time 15 minutes,
plus standing

Cooking time 15–20 minutes

2 cups chickpea (besan) flour

1 teaspoon baking powder

½ teaspoon salt

2 cups lukewarm water

¼ cup extra virgin olive oil

1 small red onion, sliced into rings

3 oz sliced salami or chorizo

10 cherry tomatoes, halved

¼ cup dairy-free herb and garlic cream
cheese or 4 oz dairy-free mozzarella
cheese alternative, sliced into chunks

This is a popular street food in Italy that is dairy-free and made with gluten-free chickpea flour. It can loosely be described as a type of pancake and comes topped with slices of salami, cherry tomatoes, red onion, and dairy-free cheese, but feel free to add your own favorite toppings.

1 Mix together the chickpea flour, baking powder, and salt in a large bowl and make a well in the center. Gradually pour the measured water and half the olive oil into the dry ingredients, whisking continuously to form a light batter. Cover and let stand for 2 hours or overnight in the refrigerator.

2 Pour the remaining olive oil into a 12 x 10 inch baking pan and place in a preheated oven, at 425°F, for 5 minutes, until hot.

3 Carefully remove the baking pan from the oven and pour the batter into the pan. Sprinkle the red onion, salami, or chorizo and tomatoes over the top, then add teaspoonfuls of the cream cheese or the mozzarella chunks. Bake for 15–20 minutes, until set and golden around the edges. Let stand for a couple of minutes before cutting into wedges.

cheesy corn muffins

Makes 6

Preparation time 15 minutes

Cooking time 20 minutes

¼ cup dairy-free spread, melted, plus extra for greasing

¾ cup instant grits or polenta

⅓ cup all-purpose flour

1 teaspoon baking powder

½ teaspoon baking soda

½ teaspoon salt

1 teaspoon dry English mustard

1 extra-large egg, lightly beaten

⅓ cup dairy-free yogurt

½ cup unsweetened dairy-free milk

½ red bell pepper, cored, seeded, and diced

½ cup shredded dairy-free cheddar cheese alternative

1 Lightly grease a 6-cup muffin pan.

2 Mix together the grits or polenta, flour, baking powder, baking soda, salt, and dry mustard in a bowl. Whisk together the egg, yogurt, milk, and melted spread in a small bowl, then pour into the dry ingredients and add the red bell pepper and cheese. Using a wooden spoon, stir together until just combined.

3 Spoon the batter evenly into the prepared muffin pan and smooth the tops. Place in a preheated oven, at 375°F, for 20 minutes, until risen and a toothpick inserted into the centers comes out clean. Transfer to a wire rack to cool. Serve warm or cold.

date & nut snack balls

Makes 12

Preparation time 15 minutes, plus chilling

⅓ cup cashew nuts

⅓ cup hazelnuts

1 tablespoon sunflower seeds

finely grated zest of 1 orange

3 tablespoons orange juice

4 dried dates

1 heaping tablespoon unsweetened
  cocoa powder, plus extra for dusting

3 tablespoons flaked unsweetened
  dried coconut

These are just the thing when only something sweet will do. These bite-size snack balls are packed with nutritious, energy-sustaining nuts, seeds, and fruit.

1 Put the nuts and seeds in a food processor and grind to a coarse powder. Transfer the mixture to a bowl and stir in the orange zest.

2 Put the orange juice and dates into the processor and blend to a puree, scraping down the sides of the small bowl, if necessary. Add the date mixture to the ground nuts and seeds, then stir in the cocoa powder and combine to form a coarse paste.

3 Place some extra cocoa powder and the coconut on separate plates. Shape the date mixture into 12 walnut-size balls, then roll half in the cocoa powder and half in the coconut until they are all evenly coated.

4 Transfer the balls to a plate, cover, and chill for 1 hour before serving. Store in an airtight container in the refrigerator for up to 1 week.

Hints and tips
You could use raw cacao powder instead of the cocoa, if you can find it.

weekdays

creamy tomato & lentil soup

Serves 4

Preparation time 15 minutes

Cooking time 30 minutes

1 tablespoon extra virgin olive oil

1 large onion, chopped

2 carrots, sliced

1 celery stick, sliced

½ cup split red lentils, rinsed

2 bay leaves

1 (28 oz) can tomato puree or
tomato sauce

2½ cups vegetable broth, plus
extra if needed (optional)

1 teaspoon dried oregano

½ teaspoon Worcestershire sauce

3 tablespoons oat cream or other
dairy-free cream

salt and black pepper

To serve

crispy fried onions

nutritional yeast flakes

This creamy and filling main meal soup is pureed until smooth, disguising the lentils and vegetables. Serve it with crusty bread.

1 Heat the oil in a large saucepan over medium heat, add the onion, carrots, and celery, cover, and sauté for 7 minutes, until softened, stirring occasionally to prevent the vegetables from sticking to the bottom of the pan.

2 Stir in the lentils and bay leaves, then the tomato puree or sauce, broth, and oregano and bring to a boil. Reduce the heat to low, cover, and simmer for 20 minutes or until the vegetables and lentils are tender.

3 Using an immersion blender, blend the soup until smooth. Stir in the Worcestershire sauce and season to taste. Add the oat cream and a little extra broth or water, if necessary.

4 Ladle into bowls and serve sprinkled with crispy fried onions and yeast flakes.

carrot pancakes

Serves 4

Preparation time 20 minutes, plus standing

Cooking time 12 minutes

8 carrots (about 1 lb), shredded

3 scallions, finely chopped

2 large handfuls of cilantro leaves, chopped

¾ cup chickpea (besan) flour, sifted

8 eggs

sunflower oil, for frying

salt and black pepper

To serve

1 quantity Dairy-Free Tzatziki (*see* page 136)

arugula leaves (optional)

1 Combine the carrots, scallions, and cilantro in a bowl with the chickpea flour. Beat 4 of the eggs in a small bowl, season, and add to the carrot mixture. Stir, then let stand for 10 minutes.

2 Heat enough oil to coat the bottom of a large skillet over medium heat, add 4 tablespoons of the batter to make 4 pancakes, flattening each with a spatula until about 3¼ inches across, and cook for 2 minutes on each side or until set and golden. Remove from the pan, blot on paper towels, and keep warm in a low oven. Repeat with the remaining batter to make 12 pancakes.

3 Meanwhile, bring a large sauté pan of water to a simmer. Break 1 of the remaining eggs into a cup. Swirl the water and slip the egg into the pan, then repeat with the remaining eggs. Simmer, occasionally spooning the water over the top of the eggs, until the whites are set but the yolks remain runny.

4 Top each serving of pancakes with a poached egg and a few spoonfuls of the tzatziki. Serve with arugula leaves, if desired.

fish, potato & corn chowder

Serves 4

Preparation time 20 minutes

Cooking time 20 minutes

1 tablespoon dairy-free spread

1 tablespoon olive oil

1 large onion, chopped

1 large celery stick, thinly sliced

1 large carrot, cut into large cubes

1 large leek, trimmed, cleaned and sliced

1 lb fish fillet, such as cod, halibut, or salmon

1 fish bouillon cube

2 bay leaves

6 Yukon gold potatoes (about 1½ lb), peeled and cut into bite-size cubes

1⅓ cups corn kernels

1 cup unsweetened dairy-free milk

¼ cup dairy-free cream cheese

handful of parsley leaves, chopped

salt and black pepper

crusty bread, to serve

Soups make a perfect warming, filling midweek meal. Stir in the dairy-free cream cheese right at the end to prevent it from curdling in the heat of the soup.

1 Heat the spread and oil in a large, heavy saucepan over medium heat, add the onion, celery, carrot, and leek, and sauté for 5 minutes, stirring frequently, until softened.

2 Meanwhile, put the fish into a large sauté pan or skillet and pour over enough water to cover. Bring almost to a boil, then turn off the heat and let stand for 5 minutes, until the fish is just cooked through. Using a spatula, remove the fish from the pan and let cool slightly.

3 Strain the fish cooking water into a small bowl and pour in extra hot water, if necessary, to make it up to 4 cups. Stir in the fish bouillon cube until dissolved.

4 Add the bay leaves to the sautéed vegetables, pour in the fish broth, and bring to a boil, then add the potatoes. Reduce the heat and simmer for 10 minutes, until the potatoes are almost tender.

5 Meanwhile, remove the skin and any bones from the fish and flake the fish into large pieces.

6 Add the corn and milk to the potatoes and simmer for 3 minutes. Add the fish and cook for another 2 minutes, until the fish is heated through, then season.

7 Remove the pan from the heat and stir in the cream cheese and parsley. Ladle into large bowls and serve with crusty bread.

refried bean tacos

Serves 4

Preparation time 20 minutes

Cooking time 10 minutes

1 (15 oz) can kidney beans in chili sauce

1 (15 oz) can kidney beans, rinsed and drained

1 small red onion, sliced

1 large garlic clove, sliced

1 tablespoon olive oil

1 teaspoon smoked paprika

1 teaspoon dried oregano

8 corn taco shells

shredded crisp lettuce

2 tomatoes, diced

mixed salad, to serve

Guacamole

2 avocadoes, halved, pitted, peeled, and sliced

1 large garlic clove, crushed

juice of 1 lime

salt and black pepper

Homemade refried beans are quick and easy to make, so they are ideal for a weekday meal. Simply serve them with a mixed salad.

1 Mash together all the guacamole ingredients, using the back of a fork, until smooth. Season to taste, cover, and set aside.

2 Put the kidney beans in chili sauce, half the drained kidney beans, the red onion, and garlic in a food processor or blender and blend together until almost smooth. Transfer the mixture to a large skillet with the remaining kidney beans, olive oil, paprika, and oregano. Season and heat through for 5–7 minutes, stirring frequently and adding a splash of water, if necessary.

3 Meanwhile, stand the taco shells on a baking sheet and place in a preheated oven, at 350°F, for 2–3 minutes, until warmed through.

4 Spoon a little shredded lettuce into each taco, then top with the bean mixture and a good spoonful of guacamole. Sprinkle with the tomato and serve with a mixed salad.

chicken cashew curry

Serves 4

Preparation time 20 minutes

Cooking time 30 minutes

¾ cup unsalted cashew nuts

1¼ cups water

1 tablespoon sunflower oil

1 onion, finely chopped

3 garlic cloves, crushed

1½ inch piece of fresh ginger root, peeled and finely grated

1 teaspoon ground cumin

2 teaspoons ground coriander

1 teaspoon turmeric

1 tablespoon garam masala

½ teaspoon mild chili powder, or to taste (optional)

1 lb boneless, skinless chicken breasts, cut into large chunks

¼ cup dairy-free yogurt, preferably unsweetened

salt and black pepper

To serve

10 cherry tomatoes, quartered

handful of fresh cilantro, chopped

cooked brown long-grain rice

1 Put the cashew nuts into a large, dry skillet and toast over medium-low heat for 5 minutes, turning once, until golden. Remove from the heat and let cool. Put the nuts into a grinder or mini food processor with ½ cup of the measured water and blend to a smooth paste.

2 Heat the oil in a saucepan over medium-low heat, add the onion, cover, and cook for 8 minutes, stirring occasionally, until soft. Add the garlic and ginger and cook for another 1 minute.

3 Stir in the spices, ground cashews, and remaining measured water and bring to a boil. Add the chicken, then reduce the heat and simmer, partly covered, for 15 minutes or until the chicken is cooked through and the sauce has reduced and thickened. Season to taste and stir in the yogurt. Top with the tomatoes and cilantro and serve with rice.

lentil & squash dhal

Serves 4

Preparation time 15 minutes

Cooking time 30 minutes

2 tablespoons sunflower oil or coconut oil

1 large onion, diced

2 large garlic cloves, finely chopped

1 inch piece of unpeeled fresh ginger
  root, grated

1 cup bite-size peeled and seeded
  butternut squash chunks

⅔ cup split red lentils, rinsed

2½ cups water

2 heaping tablespoons mild curry paste

1 teaspoon turmeric

½ teaspoon dried red pepper flakes
  (optional)

½ cup coconut milk

salt and black pepper

To serve

4 large hard-boiled eggs, shelled
  and halved

¼ cup Dairy-Free Raita (*see* page 136)

whole-grain chapattis or other flatbreads,
  warmed, or brown long-grain rice

This is a great introduction to Indian food, because it is mildly spiced yet still full of flavor. The coconut milk also helps to temper the heat from the spices as well as add a delicious creaminess. It can be served on its own with Indian breads or topped with a hard-boiled egg.

1 Heat the oil in a large, heavy saucepan over medium heat, add the onion, cover, and cook for 8 minutes, stirring occasionally, until softened. Add the garlic, ginger, and squash, then stir in the lentils and measured water.

2 Bring to a boil, then reduce the heat and stir in the curry paste, turmeric, and red pepper flakes, if using. Simmer, partly covered, for 20 minutes or until the squash and lentils are tender.

3 Using an immersion blender, blend the dhal until smooth, then stir in the coconut milk, season to taste, and reheat briefly.

4 Spoon the dhal into large serving bowls and top each portion with a hard-boiled egg and some raita. Serve with warm chapattis or other flatbreads or rice.

turkey burritos

Serves 4

Preparation time 20 minutes

Cooking time 25–30 minutes

1 cup brown long-grain rice

1 teaspoon turmeric

1 tablespoon olive oil

2 red onions, sliced

2 garlic cloves, chopped

1 (14½ oz) can diced tomatoes

1 (15 oz) can kidney beans, rinsed and drained

1 cup water

1 teaspoon ground coriander

1 teaspoon ground cumin

1 teaspoon smoked paprika

2 cups cooked turkey strips

To serve

4 large soft tortillas

¾ cup shredded dairy-free cheddar cheese alternative

1 quantity Guacamole (see page 45)

mixed salad

Making these delicious burritos is an excellent way of using up leftover cooked meat, such as turkey, chicken, pork, or beef, from the Sunday dinner.

1 Put the rice in a saucepan and add enough water to cover by ¾ inch. Stir in the turmeric and bring to a boil, then reduce the heat to its lowest setting, cover, and simmer for 20–25 minutes, until the rice is tender and the water has been absorbed. Turn off the heat and let the rice stand for 5 minutes.

2 Meanwhile, heat the oil in a separate large, heavy saucepan and cook three-quarters of the onions for 6 minutes, until softened. Stir in the garlic and cook for another 1 minute.

3 Add the tomatoes, kidney beans, and measured water and bring to a boil. Reduce the heat, stir in the spices, and cook, partly covered, for 15 minutes, until the sauce has reduced and thickened. Stir in the turkey and heat through until piping hot.

4 To serve, warm the tortillas, 2 at a time, in a large, dry skillet. Place a few spoonfuls of the rice on each tortilla and top with the sauce. Finally, top with the cheese, the remaining red onion, and a spoonful of guacamole. Fold the tortilla over the filling and serve with the remaining rice and a mixed salad.

Hints and tips

For vegetarians, eggplants, tofu, or mushrooms would work well in place of turkey.

ham fritters with salsa

Serves 4

Preparation time 15 minutes

Cooking time 25 minutes

1⅔ cups corn kernels

3 slices of thickly cut, good-quality cured ham (about 8 oz), diced

1 cup cooked rice

½ cup all-purpose flour

2 eggs, lightly beaten

⅓ cup unsweetened dairy-free milk

sunflower oil, for frying

Pineapple salsa

½ small pineapple, skinned, cored, and diced

½ red onion, diced

1 red chile, seeded and diced (optional)

juice of ½ lime

handful of cilantro leaves, chopped

salt and black pepper

1 Mix together all the salsa ingredients in a bowl, season with salt and black pepper, and set aside.

2 Put the corn kernels, ham, cooked rice, and flour into a bowl and mix together. Whisk together the eggs and milk in a small bowl, then pour into the corn mixture and stir until combined.

3 Heat enough oil to coat the bottom of a skillet over medium heat, drop in 4 large tablespoons of the mixture to make 4 fritters, and cook for 3 minutes on each side or until set and lightly golden. Remove from the pan, drain on paper towels, and keep warm in a low oven. Repeat with the remaining batter to make 16 fritters.

4 Serve the fritters with the pineapple salsa.

sesame chicken nuggets

Serves 4

Preparation time 15 minutes, plus marinating

Cooking time 20 minutes

¼ cup reduced-sodium soy sauce

2 tablespoons honey

2 tablespoons sesame oil

1¼ lb boneless, skinless chicken breasts, cut into thick long strips

olive oil, for greasing

1½ cups sesame seeds

Chili-mayo dip

⅓ cup dairy-free mayonnaise

3 tablespoons sweet chili sauce

1 tablespoon lemon juice

To serve (optional)

roasted sweet potato fries

steamed sliced carrots

A healthier version of ever-popular chicken nuggets, these are coated in calcium-rich sesame seeds and then baked in the oven until crisp and golden. The nuggets can be served with sweet potato wedges and favorite vegetables, or with a vegetable noodle stir-fry.

1 Mix together the soy sauce, honey, and sesame oil in a large, shallow dish. Add the chicken and turn to coat in the marinade, then cover and let marinate in the refrigerator for at least 30 minutes.

2 Lightly oil 2 large baking sheets. Put the sesame seeds on a large plate and roll each chicken strip in the sesame seeds until evenly coated, then transfer to the prepared baking sheets.

3 Place in a preheated oven, at 350°F, for 20 minutes, turning once, until the chicken is cooked through and the seeds are golden.

4 Meanwhile, mix together all the chili-mayo dip ingredients in a bowl.

5 Serve the chicken nuggets with the chili-mayo dip and accompanied by roasted sweet potato fries and sliced steamed carrots, if desired.

love-it linguine

Serves 4

Preparation time 5 minutes

Cooking time 15 minutes

12 oz dried linguine pasta

4 tablespoons dairy-free spread

4 teaspoons yeast extract

4 heaping teaspoons nutritional yeast flakes

black pepper

2 tablespoons toasted pine nuts, to serve

This pasta dish is so quick to make it could be served as an after-school snack as well as a speedy dinner.

1 Cook the pasta in a large saucepan of boiling water according to the package directions until al dente. Drain, reserving ½ cup of the cooking water.

2 Return the pasta to the pan with half of the reserved cooking water and place on the still-warm stove. Add the spread, yeast extract, and yeast flakes and toss until combined, adding more of the cooking water to loosen the pasta, if necessary. Season with black pepper and serve sprinkled with pine nuts.

Hints and tips

Serve the linguine topped with a fried egg and, of course, plenty of veg for a more substantial meal.

tomato pesto orzo

Serves 4

**Preparation time 15 minutes,
  plus soaking**

Cooking time 25 minutes

1 (3½ oz) package sun-dried tomatoes

2 red bell peppers, cored, seeded, and
  cut into long wedges

½ cup extra virgin olive oil, plus extra
  for brushing

¾ cup cashew nuts

2 garlic cloves, crushed

12 oz dried orzo pasta

salt and black pepper

handful of basil leaves, torn, to garnish

1 Put the sun-dried tomatoes into a heatproof bowl, cover with just-boiled water, and soak for 30 minutes, until softened.

2 Meanwhile, lightly brush both sides of the bell peppers with oil and cook under a preheated hot broiler for 15 minutes, turning once, until softened and the skins have started to blacken. Put the bell peppers into a bowl, cover with plastic wrap, and let stand until cool enough to handle; this will make the bell peppers easier to peel.

3 While the bell peppers are broiling, put the cashew nuts into a large, dry skillet and toast over medium-low heat for 5 minutes, tossing the pan occasionally, until the cashews smell toasted and start to brown. Put the nuts into a bowl and let cool, then coarsely chop.

4 Peel the skins off the bell peppers and discard. Drain the tomatoes, reserving the soaking water. Put the tomatoes into a food processor or a blender with the bell peppers, ½ cup of the soaking liquid, and the oil, then blend until smooth. Put the tomato mixture into a bowl with ½ cup of the cashews and the garlic, season to taste, and stir until combined. Set aside.

5 Cook the pasta in a large saucepan of boiling water according to the package directions. Drain the pasta, reserving ⅓ cup of the cooking water.

6 Return the pasta to the pan and spoon in enough of the pesto to coat. Add the pasta cooking water to loosen the sauce and toss until combined. Serve sprinkled with the remaining cashews and the basil leaves. Store any leftover pesto in a sealable jar in the refrigerator for up to 10 days.

creamy tomato & tuna pasta

Serves 4

Preparation time 15 minutes

Cooking time 15 minutes

2 large garlic cloves, chopped

1 tablespoon olive oil

1 (14½ oz) can diced tomatoes

½ cup water

1 tablespoon ketchup

¾ cup drained pitted black ripe olives

1 teaspoon dried oregano

1 (5 oz) can tuna in olive oil, separated into large flakes and oil reserved

2 tablespoons dairy-free cream cheese

12 oz dried tagliatelle pasta

black pepper

handful of chopped flat-leaf parsley leaves, to garnish

1 Heat the garlic in the oil in a medium saucepan, then stir in the tomatoes, measured water, ketchup, olives, and oregano. Bring almost to a boil, then reduce the heat and simmer, partly covered, for 10 minutes, until the sauce has reduced and thickened. Add the tuna with its oil, then stir in the cream cheese and cook briefly until heated through. Season with black pepper.

2 Meanwhile, cook the pasta in a large saucepan of boiling water according to the package directions. Drain, reserving ¼ cup of the water, and return the pasta to the pan.

3 Toss the sauce with the pasta and reserved cooking water. Garnish with the chopped parsley and serve.

mac with no cheese

Serves 4

Preparation time 15 minutes

Cooking time 20 minutes

12 oz dried macaroni or pasta shells

1 teaspoon vegetable bouillon powder

1 cup shredded dairy-free cheddar
cheese alternative

1¼ quantities Dairy-Free White Sauce
(*see* page 138)

2 tomatoes, sliced

1 tablespoon olive oil

1½ cups coarse fresh bread crumbs

2 garlic cloves, finely chopped

steamed peas and carrots, to serve

This dairy-free version of a popular family meal is topped with a mouth-watering layer of crispy garlicky crumbs.

1 Cook the pasta in a large saucepan of boiling water according to the package directions. Drain, then transfer the pasta to an ovenproof dish.

2 Stir the bouillon powder and cheese into the white sauce and heat through, stirring, until the cheese has melted into the sauce. Spoon the sauce over the pasta and mix until well combined. Place the slices of tomato on top and cook under a preheated medium-hot broiler for a few minutes, until the tomato has softened and is starting to brown.

3 Meanwhile, heat the oil in a large skillet over medium heat, add the bread crumbs, and cook for 3 minutes, until golden and crisp. Reduce the heat slightly, add the garlic, and cook for another 1 minute, stirring to prevent the garlic from burning.

4 Sprinkle the macaroni with the garlicky crumbs and serve with steamed peas and carrots.

baked pasta & sausages

Serves 4

Preparation time 15 minutes

Cooking time 35–40 minutes

6 good-quality herb sausage links

1 tablespoon olive oil

2 large garlic cloves, finely chopped

1½ (14½ oz) cans diced tomatoes

1 tablespoon tomato paste

12 oz dried penne pasta

3 tablespoons dairy-free garlic and herb cream cheese

1 cup shredded dairy-free mozzarella cheese alternative

This delicious pasta dish can be made in advance up to the end of step 4, then simply baked in the oven just before serving.

1 Squeeze the meat out of the sausage skins and shape into small balls—you'll get about 5 balls per sausage. Heat the oil in a large saucepan over medium heat and cook the sausage balls for 5 minutes, turning occasionally, until browned all over. Remove the sausage balls with a slotted spoon and set aside.

2 Add the garlic, tomatoes, and tomato paste to the pan, reduce the heat to medium-low, and bring to a boil. Reduce the heat to low and simmer, partly covered, for 10 minutes, stirring frequently, until reduced and thickened.

3 Meanwhile, cook the pasta in a large saucepan of boiling water according to the package directions. Drain, reserving ¼ cup of the cooking water, and return the pasta and reserved cooking water to the pan.

4 Stir the sausage balls, tomato sauce, and cream cheese into the pasta and warm through. Pour into a medium ovenproof dish and sprinkle the mozzarella over the top.

5 Cover with a lid or aluminum foil and bake in a preheated oven, at 375°F, for 10 minutes, then remove the foil and cook for another 10 minutes, until starting to brown on top.

lamb, quinoa & mint patties

Serves 4

Preparation time 20 minutes

Cooking time 16 minutes

1 lb ground lamb

2 teaspoons ground coriander

1 teaspoon ground cumin

1 teaspoon paprika

1 teaspoon dried mint

½ teaspoon dried red pepper flakes (optional)

2 garlic cloves, crushed

½ cup cooked quinoa or bulgur wheat

olive oil, for frying and drizzling

salt and black pepper

To serve

2 tomatoes, seeded and diced

1 small red onion, sliced

handful of mint leaves, coarsely chopped

1 quantity Tahini Dip (*see* page 137) or dairy-free mayonnaise

4 flatbreads

1 Mix together the lamb, spices, mint, red pepper flakes, if using, garlic, and cooked grain in a bowl and season. Using wet hands, shape the mixture into 12 patties, each about 2 inches across.

2 Heat a large ridged grill pan over high heat, then reduce the heat slightly and brush one side of the patties with oil. Grill half the patties, oil side down, for 4 minutes. Brush the tops of the patties with a little extra oil, then turn them over and cook for another 4 minutes, until golden and cooked through. Remove from the grill and cover with aluminum foil. Keep warm in the bottom of a low oven while you cook the remaining patties.

3 Meanwhile, mix together the tomatoes, onion, and mint in a serving bowl and drizzle with a little oil. Set aside. Put the tahini dip or mayonnaise in a separate serving bowl. Wrap the flatbreads in aluminum foil and warm through in the low oven.

4 Put the patties on a serving plate and let everyone help themselves to the flatbreads, patties, and toppings.

tofu steaks with egg rice

Serves 4

Preparation time 20 minutes,
plus marinating

Cooking time 25 minutes

3 tablespoons hoisin sauce

1 tablespoon sesame oil, plus extra
to serve

1 tablespoon reduced-sodium soy sauce,
plus extra to serve

13 oz firm tofu, drained, patted dry, and
cut into 8 slices

1 tablespoon sunflower oil or coconut
oil, plus extra for greasing

1 cup frozen peas

6 scallions, thinly sliced

1 red bell pepper, cored, seeded, and
thinly sliced

1 inch piece of fresh ginger root, peeled
and finely chopped

1 cup finely shredded green cabbage

2 garlic cloves, finely chopped

2 cups cooked brown long-grain rice

4 eggs

pepper

If you're using leftover rice to make this
dish, do make sure it is heated through really
thoroughly before serving. Alternatively,
cook about 1 cup dried rice, then refresh
under cold running water.

1 Mix together the hoisin sauce, sesame oil, and soy sauce in a
shallow dish. Add the tofu and spoon the marinade over until
coated. Let marinate for at least 30 minutes.

2 Lightly oil a large baking sheet. Turn the tofu in the marinade,
then arrange the slices on the baking sheet. Place in a preheated
oven, at 375°F, for 25 minutes, turning once, or until golden and
starting to crisp.

3 Meanwhile, cook the peas in a small saucepan of boiling water
for 3–4 minutes, then drain.

4 Heat the sunflower or coconut oil in a large wok or skillet, add
5 of the scallions, the red bell pepper, ginger, and green cabbage
and stir-fry for 3 minutes, until softened. Add the garlic and
rice and stir-fry for 3 minutes, until the rice is piping hot.

5 Make a hole in the center of the rice and crack in the eggs,
then cook for a minute or so, until they start to set. Start to
fold the eggs into the rice so they cook in large flakes—about
2–3 minutes. Season with black pepper, add a good splash of
sesame oil and soy sauce, and stir in the peas. Turn the rice
again and serve sprinkled with the remaining scallion and
topped with the tofu.

peanutty noodles

Serves 4

Preparation time 15 minutes

Cooking time 10 minutes

1 tablespoon sunflower oil or coconut oil

2 cups sliced white mushrooms

2 garlic cloves

1 quantity Satay Dip (*see* page 28)

3 cups small broccoli florets

1 lb cooked udon noodles

½ cup water

2 scallions, thinly sliced diagonally

3 tablespoons roasted unsalted peanuts, coarsely chopped

Noodles are always loved by kids and this dish will hopefully become a family favorite. It uses thick udon noodles, but you could use egg or whole-wheat noodles instead.

1 Heat the oil in a large wok or skillet, add the mushrooms, and stir-fry for 7 minutes, until soft and starting to crisp. Add the garlic and cook for another 1 minute, then stir in the satay dip.

2 Meanwhile, steam the broccoli for 5 minutes, until just tender, then refresh under cold running water.

3 Add the noodles to the satay mushrooms, separating them with your fingers, then reduce the heat to low and add the measured water and broccoli. Heat through until piping hot, adding a splash more water, if necessary.

4 Serve the noodles sprinkled with the scallions and peanuts.

Hints and tips
For a more substantial meal, you could also top the noodles with cubes of smoked tofu, slices of omelet, or cooked shrimp.

salmon & potato tortilla

Serves 3–4

Preparation time 15 minutes

Cooking time 30–40 minutes

3 tablespoons olive oil

4 red-skinned or white round potatoes (about 1 lb), peeled and cubed

1 large onion, sliced

⅔ cup frozen baby peas

1 (7½ oz) can red salmon, drained, skin and bones removed, and fish flaked

6 extra-large eggs, lightly beaten

1 tablespoon dairy-free spread

salt and black pepper

1 Heat the oil in a medium ovenproof skillet over medium heat. Reduce the heat, add the potatoes, and cook for 15–20 minutes, turning occasionally, until tender. Remove with a slotted spoon and transfer to a bowl.

2 Pour off all but 1 tablespoon of the oil, reduce the heat slightly, and add the onion to the pan. Cook for 8 minutes, stirring occasionally, until softened.

3 Meanwhile, steam the peas until tender, then add to the bowl with the potatoes. Add the cooked onion, salmon, and eggs to the bowl, season with salt and black pepper, and turn gently until combined.

4 Wipe out the skillet, then melt the spread over medium-low heat. Pour in the egg mixture in an even layer, making sure the potatoes, peas, onion, and salmon are evenly distributed. Cook for 6–8 minutes, until the bottom is light golden and set, then place under a preheated medium broiler and cook for 2–3 minutes, until the top is just set. Serve cut into wedges.

bbq mushroom burgers

Serves 4

Preparation time 15 minutes,
 plus marinating

Cooking time 20–25 minutes

¼ cup ketchup

2 tablespoons reduced-sodium soy sauce

1 tablespoon balsamic vinegar

1 tablespoon honey or maple syrup

1 tablespoon olive oil

4 large flat mushrooms, wiped clean
 and stems removed

⅓ cup drained and coarsely chopped
 silken tofu

To serve

3 tomatoes, seeded and diced

2 scallions, finely chopped

½ red bell pepper, cored, seeded,
 and diced

shredded crisp lettuce

4 soft seeded whole-grain rolls,
 halved and lightly toasted

Barbecue sauce is simple to make and adds a wonderful flavor and color to these simple mushroom burgers.

1 Mix together the ketchup, soy sauce, vinegar, honey or maple syrup, and oil in a bowl. Brush two-thirds of the barbecue sauce all over the mushrooms, then transfer the mushrooms to a roasting pan. Place in a preheated oven, at 400°F), for 20–25 minutes or until tender.

2 Meanwhile, add the tofu to the remaining barbecue sauce and blend with an immersion blender until smooth and thick.

3 Mix together the tomatoes, scallions, and red bell pepper in a bowl. Place some shredded lettuce on top of the toasted roll bottoms. Top each with a mushroom, then add a spoonful each of the creamy barbecue sauce and tomato relish. Top with the roll lids and serve.

sausage & broccoli tart

Serves 4

Preparation time 15 minutes

Cooking time 40 minutes

1 tablespoon olive oil, plus extra for greasing and brushing

1 onion, thinly sliced

1 large garlic clove, thinly sliced

½ cup tomato puree or tomato sauce

1 tablespoon tomato paste

1 teaspoon dried thyme

1 sheet dairy-free ready-to-bake puff pastry

4 herb pork sausage links

beaten egg, to glaze

3 cups small broccoli florets

salt and black pepper

Most store-bought puff pastry is dairy-free, but it always pays to check the packaging—you obviously want to avoid the "all-butter" versions. This is a simple tart to make and just needs the addition of new potatoes and vegetables.

1 Lightly grease a large baking sheet.

2 Heat the oil in a large skillet over medium-low heat, add the onion, and cook for 10 minutes, until softened, reducing the heat if the onion starts to brown. Stir in the garlic 1 minute before the end of the cooking time, then remove the pan from the heat.

3 Mix together the tomato puree or sauce, tomato paste, and thyme in a bowl, then season with salt and black pepper.

4 Unroll the sheet of pastry and place it on the prepared baking sheet. Score a border about ½ inch in from the edge and roll the edges up slightly. Spread the tomato mixture over the pastry within the border. Spoon the onion over the top in an even layer.

5 Squeeze the meat out of the sausage skins, form into bite-size balls, and place evenly over the tart. Brush the balls with oil, then brush the edges of the pastry with egg. Place in a preheated oven, at 400°F, for 20 minutes.

6 Meanwhile, steam the broccoli florets until just tender. Arrange the broccoli on top of the tart, brush with a little oil, and return to the oven for another 10 minutes or until the pastry is cooked and golden.

chorizo & bean stew with mashed sweet potatoes

Serves 4

Preparation time 15 minutes

Cooking time 25 minutes

1 tablespoon olive oil

1 large onion, chopped

8 oz chorizo sausage, skin removed and cut into bite-size chunks

2 garlic cloves, chopped

1 teaspoon dried oregano

1 (14½ oz) can diced tomatoes

1 tablespoon tomato paste

1 teaspoon smoked paprika

1 (15 oz) can baked beans

salt and black pepper

chopped fresh cilantro, to garnish

Mashed sweet potatoes

4–5 sweet potatoes (about 1½ lb), peeled and cut into large chunks

1 large garlic clove, sliced

2–3 tablespoons dairy-free mayonnaise

This stew has a real Spanish feel, despite the addition of baked beans.

1 Heat the oil in a large, heavy saucepan over medium heat, add the onion, and cook for 6 minutes, stirring frequently, until softened. Stir in the chorizo and cook for another 3 minutes. Add the garlic and continue to cook for 1 minute.

2 Add the oregano, tomatoes, tomato paste, and smoked paprika. Fill the empty tomato can one-third full with water, swill it around, and add the liquid to the pan. Bring to a boil, then reduce the heat and simmer, partly covered, for 10 minutes, until the sauce has reduced and thickened. Stir in the beans, season with salt and black pepper, and heat through.

3 Meanwhile, make the mashed sweet potatoes. Cook the sweet potatoes and garlic in a saucepan of boiling water for 12–15 minutes, until tender, then drain and return the potatoes to the pan to dry. Add the mayonnaise and mash until smooth.

4 Serve the stew, sprinkled with cilantro, with the mashed sweet potatoes.

Hints and tips
You could, of course, replace the beans with a can of chickpeas or another favorite bean and increase the quantity of canned tomatoes by ¾ cup.

omelet "pizzas"

Serves 2

Preparation time 10 minutes

Cooking time 10 minutes

1½ tablespoons dairy-free spread

4 eggs

½ small red onion, thinly sliced into rings

1 tomato, seeded and diced

2 mushrooms, thinly sliced

handful of pitted olives, halved

2 teaspoons dairy-free pesto, or
   homemade Tomato Pesto (*see* page 53)

2 tablespoons dairy-free cream cheese or
   grated mozzarella cheese alternative

extra virgin olive oil, for drizzling

1 Heat half the spread in a medium ovenproof skillet over medium heat. Lightly beat 2 of the eggs in a bowl, then pour into the pan. Turn the pan until the eggs coat the bottom in an even layer, then cook until the bottom of the omelet is set but the top is still slightly runny.

2 Arrange half the onion, tomato, mushrooms, and olives over the top. Dot half the pesto and cheese on top, then drizzle with a little oil. Place under a preheated medium broiler and cook for 2 minutes or until just cooked. Keep warm in a low oven.

3 Repeat with the remaining ingredients to make a second "pizza." Slip onto a serving plate and serve hot.

weekends

summer rolls

Makes 12

Preparation time 20 minutes

Cooking time 3 minutes

2 oz vermicelli rice noodles

1 teaspoon sesame oil

12 rice paper wrappers

3 inch piece of cucumber, seeded and cut into long, thin strips

½ red bell pepper, cored, seeded, and cut into long, thin strips

2 scallions, halved and cut into long, thin strips

6 oz large, cooked peeled shrimp, sliced in half lengthwise

1 tablespoon sesame seeds, toasted

handful of basil leaves

Dipping sauce

2 tablespoons hoisin sauce, plus extra for drizzling

1 tablespoon reduced-sodium soy sauce

juice of 1 lime

honey, to taste

Get the kids to help you make these rice paper rolls, which are filled with shrimp and fresh vegetables—have all the fillings prepared before you soak the wrappers. They are plenty of fun to make and can be served as a lunch or with a stir-fry for a more filling meal.

1 Cook the rice noodles according to the package directions, then drain and toss in the sesame oil.

2 Meanwhile, mix together all the dipping sauce ingredients in a bowl.

3 To assemble the rolls, pour hot water into a large bowl. Place a rice paper wrapper flat in the water until pliable, but not too soft. Carefully remove the wrapper from the bowl, using a spatula, and place flat on a cutting board.

4 Drizzle a little hoisin sauce horizontally near the bottom of the wrapper and top with a few strips of cucumber, red bell pepper, and scallion, 3 halves of shrimp, a sprinkling of sesame seeds, and a couple of basil leaves. (Be careful not to overfill the wrapper, because this makes it difficult to fold.)

5 Bring the bottom edge of the wrapper tightly over the filling and tuck in the sides, then continue to roll up to encase the filling. Put the rice paper roll on a plate, seam side down. Repeat with the remaining ingredients to make 12 rolls.

6 Serve the summer rolls with the dipping sauce.

beef & lentil lasagne

Serves 4–6

Preparation time 20 minutes

Cooking time 1 hour 35 minutes

2 tablespoons olive oil

1 large onion, chopped

1 carrot, diced

1 celery stick, diced

2 large garlic cloves, chopped

8 oz bacon, coarsely chopped

1 lb ground beef round or sirloin

1 cup red wine or extra broth

1 (14½ oz) can diced tomatoes

2 tablespoons tomato paste

1 cup beef broth

2 tablespoons each chopped sage, parsley, and thyme

2 bay leaves

2 cups cooked green lentils

12 fresh lasagna noodles

1 quantity Dairy-Free White Sauce (*see* page 138)

2 tablespoons crispy fried onions (optional)

salt and black pepper

We all know that we should be cutting back on the amount of meat we eat. Consequently, this delicious lasagne goes easy on the beef, but includes lentils to give it extra substance.

1 Heat half the oil in a large, heavy saucepan over medium heat, add the onion, and cook for 5 minutes, until softened. Add the carrot and celery and cook for another 5 minutes, then stir in the garlic. Remove the vegetables from the pan and set aside.

2 Add the remaining oil to the pan and cook the bacon for 5 minutes, until golden. Remove from the pan with a slotted spoon, add the ground beef, and cook for about 5 minutes, until browned. Return the onion mixture and bacon to the pan and pour in the wine or extra broth. Let it simmer for 5 minutes or until there is no aroma of alcohol.

3 Add the tomatoes, tomato paste, broth, and herbs to the pan and bring to a boil, then reduce the heat and simmer, partly covered, for 25 minutes, stirring occasionally. Add the lentils, season with salt and black pepper, and cook for another 5 minutes, until heated through; remove the lid if the sauce is too thin.

4 To assemble the lasagne, spoon one-third of the meat sauce into a 1¾ quart ovenproof dish. Top with a layer of lasagna noodles, then spread over one-third of the white sauce. Repeat with another 2 layers of meat sauce, lasagna noodles, and white sauce. Sprinkle the crispy onions over the top, if using.

5 Cook in a preheated oven, at 350°F, for 35–40 minutes, until the lasagne is cooked through.

bacon & pea tart

Serves 4

Preparation time 20 minutes

Cooking time 1 hour 5 minutes

1½ tablespoons dairy-free spread, plus extra for greasing

1 sheet store-bought rolled dough pie crust

flour, for dusting

8 smoked bacon slices

2 large onions, finely chopped

½ cup frozen baby peas

2 extra-large eggs

1 cup unsweetened almond milk (*see* page 134 for homemade) or other dairy-free milk

½ cup dairy-free cream

1 teaspoon Dijon mustard

1 tablespoon nutritional yeast flakes

1 teaspoon dried thyme

salt and black pepper

Nutritional yeast flakes can be bought in health food stores or online and make a nutritious alternative to cheese, thanks to their cheesy flavor. They are especially good in sauces because they dissolve when heated.

1 Lightly grease a 9 inch loose-bottom tart pan.

2 Roll out the dough on a lightly floured work surface and use to line the prepared tart pan. Line the pastry shell with parchment paper and pie weights or dried beans, then bake in a preheated oven, at 350°F, for 15 minutes. Remove the weights and paper and return the shell to the oven for another 15 minutes, until the pastry is crisp and light golden.

3 Meanwhile, put the bacon on an aluminum foil-lined baking sheet and place it in the oven to cook alongside the pastry shell for 15–20 minutes, turning once, until golden and starting to crisp. Drain the bacon on paper towels to remove any excess fat.

4 While the pastry shell and bacon are cooking, heat the spread in a large skillet over medium-low heat and gently cook the onions for 20 minutes, until soft, reducing the heat if they start to brown. Steam the peas in a separate saucepan until tender.

5 Whisk together the eggs, milk, cream, mustard, yeast flakes, and thyme in a small bowl, then season with salt and black pepper.

6 Spoon the onions and peas into the pastry shell in an even layer. Cut the bacon into bite-size pieces and sprinkle them over the top. Pour the egg mixture into the pastry shell and bake for 35 minutes or until just set and starting to brown.

smoked salmon & kale risotto,

Serves 4

Preparation time 15 minutes

Cooking time 40 minutes

1 tablespoon dairy-free spread

1 tablespoon olive oil

1 large onion, finely chopped

2 cups risotto rice

¾ cup dry white wine or extra broth

5 cups hot fish broth

1 cup finely chopped kale (tough stems discarded) or small broccoli florets

1 heaping tablespoon dairy-free cream cheese

5 oz smoked salmon pieces

handful of chives, snipped

juice of ½ lemon

black pepper

1 Heat the spread and oil in a large heavy saucepan over medium-low heat, add the onion, and cook gently for 10 minutes, stirring frequently, until softened but not browned. Add the rice and stir to coat it in the onion mixture.

2 Pour the wine or extra broth into the pan and let it simmer, stirring, for 5 minutes, until absorbed by the rice and there is no aroma of alcohol. Start to add the broth, a ladleful at a time, stirring continuously. Only add the next ladleful of broth when the previous one has been absorbed, and continue for about 25 minutes in total, until the rice is creamy with just a slight bite. The risotto should be slightly soupy and not dry.

3 Meanwhile, steam the kale or broccoli until tender, then refresh under cold running water.

4 When the rice is cooked, remove the pan from the heat, season with black pepper, and stir in the kale, cream cheese, smoked salmon, half the chives, and the lemon juice. Stir gently but thoroughly until combined. Cover and let stand on the warm stove for a couple of minutes to heat through. Serve sprinkled with the remaining chives.

Hints and tips

Although there is wine in this creamy salmon risotto for added flavor, the alcohol is actually burned off, so there is no trace left; however, you can use extra broth instead of the wine, if preferred.

pea & mint risotto

Serves 4

Preparation time 20 minutes

Cooking time 40 minutes

2 tablespoons olive oil

2 leeks, trimmed, cleaned and
  finely chopped

2 cups risotto rice

¾ cup dry white wine or extra broth

6⅓ cups hot vegetable broth

2 cups frozen peas

handful of mint leaves, chopped

handful of basil leaves

¼ cup nutritional yeast flakes

4 eggs

salt and black pepper

1 Heat the oil in a large, heavy saucepan, add the leeks, cover, and sauté for 5 minutes, stirring occasionally, until soft and tender. Add the rice and stir for a couple of minutes to coat it in the leek mixture.

2 Pour the wine into the pan and let simmer, stirring, for 5 minutes, until absorbed by the rice and there is no aroma of alcohol. Start to add the broth, a ladleful at a time, stirring continuously. Only add the next ladleful of broth when the previous one has been absorbed by the rice and continue for about 25 minutes in total, until the rice is creamy with just a slight bite. The rice should be slightly soupy and not dry.

3 Meanwhile, steam the peas until tender. Put them into a blender or food processor, add the mint, basil, and ½ cup of the broth, and blend until pureed, then set aside.

4 When the risotto is cooked, turn off the heat and stir in the pea puree and three-quarters of the yeast flakes. Season to taste, cover, and let stand on the warm stove until ready to serve.

5 Meanwhile, bring a large sauté pan of water to a boil, then reduce the heat to a simmer. Break an egg into a cup. Swirl the water and slip the egg into the pan, then repeat with the remaining 3 eggs. Simmer, occasionally spooning the water over the top of the eggs, until the whites are set but the yolks remain runny.

6 Top each serving of the risotto with a poached egg and serve sprinkled with the remaining yeast flakes.

thai tofu burgers

Serves 4

Preparation time 20 minutes, plus chilling

Cooking time 16 minutes

1 lb firm tofu, drained, patted dry and coarsely grated

4 teaspoons Thai red curry paste

3 garlic cloves, finely chopped

1 inch piece of fresh ginger root, peeled and grated

4 scallions, finely chopped

1½ tablespoons reduced-sodium soy sauce

1 extra-large egg white

3 tablespoons all-purpose flour

sunflower oil, for frying

black pepper

Sweet chili dip

3 tablespoons dairy-free mayonnaise

2 tablespoons sweet chili sauce

juice of ½ lime

To serve

4 mini naans or other flatbreads, warmed

1 small butterhead lettuce, shredded

2 inch piece of cucumber, sliced

1 scallion, thinly shredded

1 Put the tofu into a bowl and stir in the curry paste, garlic, ginger, scallions, soy sauce, egg white, and flour. Season with black pepper and stir thoroughly until combined. Cover and chill for about 30 minutes to let the flavors meld.

2 Using wet hands, shape the tofu mixture into 8 small patties. Heat enough oil to generously coat the bottom of a large skillet. Cook the tofu burgers, in 2 batches, for 4 minutes on each side, until golden and cooked through. Remove with a slotted spoon, drain on paper towels, and keep warm in a low oven while you cook the remaining burgers.

3 Meanwhile, make the sweet chili dip. Mix together the mayo, sweet chili sauce, and lime juice in a bowl until combined.

4 To serve, spoon the sweet chili dip over the warm naans or other flatbreads, then top with the shredded lettuce, tofu burgers, cucumber, and scallions.

Hints and tips
Tofu makes surprisingly good, nutritious burgers, but because of its mild flavor, you need to be generous with the flavorings.

coconutty fish curry

Serves 4

Preparation time 15 minutes,
  plus marinating

Cooking time 30 minutes

2 tablespoons olive oil

1 large onion, coarsely grated

3 garlic cloves, coarsely grated

1½ teaspoons turmeric

8 oz raw peeled jumbo shrimp

12 oz thick skinless, boneless white fish,
  such as halibut, red snapper, or cod
  fillets, cut into large bite-size chunks

1 inch piece of fresh ginger root, peeled
  and finely chopped

1 large red bell pepper, cored, seeded,
  and chopped

1¾ cups coconut milk

⅔ cup fish broth

1–2 teaspoons mild chili powder, to taste
  (optional)

3 tablespoons tomato paste

2 large handfuls of cilantro leaves,
  chopped

salt and black pepper

To serve

Thai jasmine rice

lime wedges

I would recommend trying this mild, creamy coconut fish curry as a great way to encourage kids to eat both seafood and spices. Serve it with steamed rice and vegetables.

1 Mix together half the oil, one-third of the onion and garlic, and half the turmeric in a large bowl. Season with salt and black pepper, then add the shrimp and fish and turn gently to coat them in the marinade. Cover and let marinate in the refrigerator for at least 30 minutes.

2 Heat the remaining oil in a medium saucepan over medium-low heat, add the remaining onion, and cook for 8 minutes, stirring frequently, until softened. Reduce the heat to low, add the remaining garlic, the ginger, and red bell pepper, and cook for 3 minutes, stirring frequently.

3 Pour in the coconut milk and broth and bring to a boil, then reduce the heat, stir in the chili powder, if using, tomato paste, and the remaining turmeric and simmer for 15 minutes, stirring occasionally, until reduced by one-third.

4 Add half the cilantro, the shrimp, fish, and marinade and cook for 3 minutes or until the shrimp have turned pink and the fish is cooked through, then season to taste.

5 Sprinkle with the remaining cilantro and serve with rice and lime wedges for squeezing over.

salmon casserole

Serves 4

Preparation time 20 minutes

Cooking time 50 minutes

7 russet potatoes (about 1¾ lb), peeled and quartered

3 tablespoons dairy-free spread

1 tablespoon olive oil

2 large leeks, trimmed, cleaned, and thinly sliced

1 cup frozen peas

2 tablespoons all-purpose flour

1 large garlic clove, finely chopped

⅔ cup dairy-free cream cheese

2 tablespoons lemon juice

2 heaping teaspoons dry English mustard

handful of parsley, finely chopped

about 1 cup unsweetened dairy-free milk

1 lb skinless salmon fillets, cut into large bite-size pieces

3 oz smoked salmon pieces

salt and black pepper

This is a great alternative Sunday dinner to the usual meat option. The casserole uses just salmon, but you could use a combination of fish.

1 Cook the potatoes in a large saucepan of salted boiling water for 10–15 minutes, until tender, then drain and return to the pan.

2 Meanwhile, heat half the spread and the oil in a large skillet over medium-low heat, add the leeks, cover, and sauté for 10 minutes, until soft but not browned.

3 Steam the peas in a separate saucepan, drain, and set aside.

4 Stir the flour into the leeks and continue to cook over low heat for 2 minutes, stirring continuously. Turn off the heat but leave the pan on the warm stove and stir in the garlic, cream cheese, lemon juice, mustard, parsley, and ¾ cup of the milk until combined. Fold in the salmon, smoked salmon, and peas and season to taste.

5 Add the remaining spread and ¼ cup milk to the potatoes. Warm briefly, then mash until smooth, adding a little extra milk, if necessary. Season to taste.

6 Spoon the salmon mixture into a 1¾ quart ovenproof dish. Top with the mashed potatoes and run a fork over the top to create a slightly rough texture. Bake in a preheated oven, at 400°F, for 30 minutes or until the salmon is cooked through and the top is golden and crisp.

piri piri chicken

Serves 4

Preparation time 15 minutes, plus marinating

Cooking time 30–40 minutes

6–8 chicken thighs, depending on their size, bone in and skin on

1 large red bell pepper, cored, seeded, and sliced

1 mild red chile, seeded and quartered (optional)

1 garlic clove, halved

1 tablespoon red wine vinegar

1 teaspoon paprika

1 tablespoon chopped flat leaf parsley leaves

salt and black pepper

To serve (optional)

roasted potato wedges

mixed salad

Serve the chicken with baked potato wedges, which can be put in the oven at the same time as the thighs, or rice and a salad. If you want to avoid the chile in the zingy red pepper marinade, you can omit it without detrimentally affecting the flavor.

1 Make 3 diagonal cuts in the skin of each chicken thigh, then transfer to a large, shallow nonreactive dish.

2 Blend together the remaining ingredients in a food processor or blender until smooth, then spoon over the chicken thighs and turn until well coated. Cover and let marinate in the refrigerator for at least 30 minutes.

3 Transfer the chicken thighs to a roasting pan and spoon any leftover sauce in the dish on top. Roast in a preheated oven, at 375°F, for 30–40 minutes or until cooked through and golden.

4 Serve with roasted potato wedges and a mixed salad, if desired.

oven-baked falafel

Serves 3–4

Preparation time 15 minutes, plus chilling

Cooking time 20–30 minutes

1 (15 oz) can chickpeas, rinsed and drained

1 small onion, quartered

2 garlic cloves, halved

1 heaping teaspoon ground cumin

2 heaping teaspoons ground coriander

1 teaspoon dried mint

½ teaspoon harissa paste (optional)

1 tablespoon extra virgin olive oil, plus
   extra for greasing and brushing

2 tablespoons chickpea (besan) flour

salt and black pepper

To serve

4 pita breads, warmed

¼ cup hummus

few drops of chili sauce (optional)

shredded butterhead lettuce

2 tomatoes, sliced

few slices of cucumber

salad greens

potato wedges

This makes a great meal for a Saturday night in front of the TV, where everyone can help themselves to the falafel, warm pita bread, and other fillings. It is much easier to bake the falafel in the oven, because they can all be cooked at once instead of fried in batches, and this also reduces the fat levels.

1 Put the chickpeas, onion, garlic, spices, mint, harissa, if using, and oil in a food processor or blender and process to a coarse paste. Stir in the chickpea flour and season. Shape the mixture into 12 patties, each about the size of a flattened golf ball. Cover and chill for 30 minutes, until firm.

2 Lightly grease a large baking sheet. Brush both sides of the falafel with oil and transfer to the sheet. Place in a preheated oven, at 375°F, and cook for 20–30 minutes, turning once, until golden and crisp.

3 Slice the warmed pita breads open and spread with the hummus, adding a splash of chili sauce, if desired. Fill each pita with lettuce, falafel, tomatoes, and cucumber. Serve with salad and potato wedges.

sweet & sour pork balls

Serves 4

Preparation time 25 minutes

Cooking time 15 minutes

2 large garlic cloves, finely chopped

1 inch piece of unpeeled fresh ginger root, grated

1 lb ground pork

2 scallions, finely chopped

2 tablespoons reduced-sodium soy sauce

½ teaspoon Chinese 5-spice powder

1 tablespoon sesame oil

1 tablespoon cornstarch

1 egg, lightly beaten

sunflower oil, for frying

12 oz whole-wheat noodles

salt and black pepper

Sweet and sour sauce

2 large garlic cloves, finely chopped

1 inch piece of unpeeled fresh ginger root, grated

1 small red bell pepper, cored, seeded, and sliced

2 tomatoes, coarsely chopped

2 tablespoons ketchup

2 tablespoons reduced-sodium soy sauce

1 tablespoon tomato paste

1 teaspoon honey

¼ cup water

1 To make the pork balls, put all the ingredients, except the sunflower oil, noodles, and sauce ingredients into a bowl. Season with salt and black pepper and stir until well combined. Using wet hands, shape the mixture into 20 walnut-size balls. Cover and put into the refrigerator until firm while you prepare the sauce.

2 Place all the sauce ingredients in a food processor or blender and blend to a puree. Set aside.

3 Heat enough oil to generously cover the bottom of a large skillet over medium heat. Cook the pork balls, in 2 batches, for 6 minutes, until browned all over and cooked through. Return all the pork balls to the pan, pour in the sweet and sour sauce, and cook for another 2–3 minutes, until heated through, adding a splash of water, if necessary.

4 Meanwhile, cook the noodles according to the package directions, then drain and divide among 4 bowls. Spoon the pork balls and sauce over the noodles and serve immediately.

pizza bombas

Makes 20

Preparation time 40 minutes, plus rising

Cooking time 25 minutes

2¼ teaspoons or 1 (¼ oz) envelope active dry yeast

2 teaspoons superfine or granulated sugar

2 tablespoons extra virgin olive oil, plus extra for oiling

1¼ cups lukewarm water

3⅔ cups white bread flour, plus extra for dusting

1½ teaspoons salt

Filling

1½ tablespoons dairy-free spread

3 cups diced cremini mushrooms

2 large garlic cloves, finely chopped

1 teaspoon dried oregano

12 medium slices of chorizo, coarsely chopped

2 tablespoons dairy-free cream cheese

Tomato sauce

2 tablespoons extra virgin olive oil

1 large garlic clove, finely chopped

1¾ cups tomato puree or tomato sauce

1 tablespoon tomato paste

½ teaspoon superfine or granulated sugar

1 teaspoon dried oregano

1 Stir together the yeast, sugar, olive oil, and measured water in a small bowl and let stand for 5 minutes. Sift the flour and salt into a large bowl and make a large well in the center. Pour the yeast mixture into the well, then gradually draw the flour mixture into the liquid, using a fork. Using your hands, combine to form a ball. Turn out the dough onto a floured work surface and knead for 10 minutes, until smooth and elastic. Put into a lightly oiled bowl, cover with plastic wrap, and let rise in a warm place for about 1½ hours, until doubled in size.

2 Meanwhile, make the filling. Heat the spread in a large skillet over medium heat, add the mushrooms, and cook for 10 minutes, until any liquid in the pan has evaporated and the mushrooms start to crisp. Remove from the heat and stir in the garlic, oregano, chorizo, and cream cheese. Set aside.

3 Make the tomato sauce. Heat the oil in a saucepan and add all the remaining ingredients. Stir and bring almost to a boil, then reduce the heat and simmer, partly covered, for 10 minutes, until reduced and thickened.

4 Divide the dough into 20 equal pieces, each about the size of a golf ball. Form a piece of dough into a flattish disk and place a heaping teaspoon of the mushroom filling in the center, then draw the sides of the dough up around the filling and press the edges together to seal into a ball. Lightly oil a large baking sheet and roll the ball in the oil until coated. Repeat with the remaining dough and filling, then let rise for 15 minutes.

5 Bake the bombas in a preheated oven, at 400°F, for 15 minutes, until risen and golden. Reheat the tomato sauce and serve with the bombas.

beef & barbecue sauce kebabs

Serves 4

Preparation time 20 minutes, plus marinating

Cooking time 8 minutes

1 lb beef tenderloin steak, cut into 32 large bite-size cubes

24 cherry tomatoes

1 large red onion, halved and cut into 16 wedges

Marinade

¼ cup tomato paste

2 tablespoons ketchup

1 teaspoon Worcestershire sauce

1 tablespoon apple cider vinegar

2 teaspoons smoked paprika

1 tablespoon olive oil, plus extra for brushing

To serve

rice, bulgur wheat, or couscous

1 quantity Dairy-Free Tzatziki (*see* page 136)

The barbecue sauce marinade gives these beef kebabs a great smokey flavor and glossy coating. The kebabs are broiled but would also taste great grilled on the barbecue.

1 Mix together all the marinade ingredients in a large, shallow nonreactive dish. Add the beef and turn until coated, then cover and let marinate in the refrigerator for at least 1 hour.

2 Starting and ending with the beef, thread the beef, cherry tomatoes, and onion wedges onto 8 metal skewers. Turn the skewers in the marinade and brush with extra oil.

3 Arrange the skewers on an aluminum foil-lined broiler rack or on a grill rack. Cook under a preheated medium-high broiler or on a grill for 8 minutes, until the vegetables are tender and the meat is just cooked through but not pink, turning occasionally and basting with more of the marinade to prevent the beef from drying out.

4 Serve the kebabs with rice, bulgur wheat, or couscous and spoonfuls of tzatziki.

creamy chicken & leek pie

Serves 4–6

Preparation time 20 minutes

Cooking time 1¼ hours

4 bacon slices

2 tablespoons olive oil

1¼ lb boneless, skinless chicken thighs,
  cut into large bite-size chunks

1 large leek, trimmed, cleaned,
  and chopped

4 cups quartered cremini mushrooms

2 large garlic cloves, finely chopped

1½ teaspoons dried thyme

1 cup chicken broth

1 tablespoon cornstarch

1 tablespoon water

2 tablespoons dairy-free cream cheese

1 sheet store-bought, ready-to-bake
  dairy-free puff pastry

flour, for dusting

a little dairy-free milk, to glaze

salt and black pepper

1 Cook the bacon under a preheated hot broiler or in a skillet until almost crisp, then drain on paper towels.

2 Meanwhile, heat half the oil in a large, heavy saucepan over medium-high heat, add half the chicken, and cook for 5 minutes, until browned all over, then remove from the pan with a slotted spoon and set aside. Repeat with the remaining chicken, adding a little of the remaining oil, if necessary, then remove from the pan.

3 Heat the remaining oil in the pan, add the leek, and cook for 5 minutes, until softened. Add the mushrooms and cook for another 5 minutes, until tender, then stir in the browned chicken, the garlic, and thyme. Pour in the broth and bring to a boil, then reduce the heat and simmer, partly covered, for 20 minutes, until reduced.

4 Stir the cornstarch into the measured water in a cup, then add to the pan and cook for 5 minutes, until the sauce has thickened, stirring frequently. Turn off the heat and stir in the cream cheese. Cut the bacon into pieces and add these to the pan, then season to taste.

5 Spoon the chicken filling into a 12 x 10 inch pie plate. Roll out the pastry on a lightly floured work surface so it is 3 inches larger than the top of the pie plate. Cut a ¾ inch-wide strip of pastry the same length as the rim of the pie plate. Brush the rim of the pie plate with water, then place the pastry strip on top. Brush the pastry strip with a little water, then place the large sheet of pastry on top. Trim and crimp the edges, then decorate the top with any surplus pastry. Brush the top with milk and prick a few times with a fork.

6 Bake in a preheated oven, at 425°F, for 30 minutes, until the pastry is golden and cooked.

pork stew with herb dumplings

Serves 4

Preparation time 25 minutes

Cooking time 1¾ hours

2 tablespoons olive oil

1½–1¾ lb shoulder or leg of pork, cut into large bite-size pieces

2 onions, sliced

2 carrots, sliced

1 cup hard dry apple cider or extra broth

2 cups chicken broth

2 bay leaves

2 teaspoons finely chopped rosemary

salt and black pepper

Herb dumplings

¾ cup all-purpose flour, plus extra for dusting

¾ teaspoon baking powder

heaping ¼ teaspoon baking soda

1 teaspoon dried thyme

1 teaspoon dry English mustard

½ cup dairy-free yogurt, preferably unsweetened

The dumplings are light and fluffy and add the finishing touch to this warming, comforting, wintry meal.

1 Heat half the oil in a large, heavy flameproof casserole or Dutch oven over medium heat, add the pork, in 2 batches, and cook for 5 minutes, until browned all over. Remove the pork from the casserole and set aside.

2 Heat the remaining oil in the casserole, add the onions, and cook for 5 minutes, until softened, then stir in the carrots and cook for another 2 minutes.

3 Pour in the cider or extra broth and let simmer until reduced by half and there is no aroma of alcohol. Pour in the broth, add the pork, bay leaves, and rosemary, and bring to a boil. Stir, then cover and transfer to a preheated oven, at 350°F, for 1 hour.

4 Meanwhile, make the herb dumplings. Mix together the flour, baking powder, baking soda, and thyme in a bowl. Stir in the mustard and yogurt, then using your hands, combine to form a ball. Divide the dough into 8 equal pieces and, using floured hands, shape into dumplings. Arrange the dumplings in the casserole so they are half submerged. Replace the lid and return to the oven for another 15 minutes, then remove the lid and continue to cook for 10 minutes, until they are light and fluffy.

picnic rolls

Makes 4

Preparation time 20 minutes, plus standing

4 crusty rolls

extra virgin olive oil, for brushing

⅓ cup dairy-free pesto, or homemade Tomato Pesto (*see* page 53)

2 handfuls of baby spinach leaves

8 slices of roasted red pepper from a jar, drained

¼ cup dairy-free cream cheese

4 thick slices of ham

The filling is hidden inside these little rolls, making them sturdy enough to transport.

1 Slice the top off each roll to form a lid and set aside. Pull out the soft bread inside the bottoms and set aside, leaving a ½ inch shell. Lightly brush the inside of each roll with oil.

2 Put the soft bread in a food processor and pulse to form bread crumbs. Mix half of the crumbs with the pesto.

3 Place a layer of spinach in the bottom of each roll and top with a layer of pesto crumbs and all the red pepper. Spread with the cream cheese and top with the ham, remaining crumbs, and spinach. Place the lids on top and wrap tightly in plastic wrap. Press down lightly and let stand for 30 minutes.

carrot & cabbage slaw

Serves 4

Preparation time 15 minutes

1½ cups shredded red cabbage

2 carrots, shredded

3 scallions, finely chopped

½ cup dairy-free yogurt, preferably unsweetened

1 teaspoon whole-grain mustard

juice of 1 small lemon

black pepper

This crisp and vibrant dairy-free version is a real improvement on the usual store-bought coleslaw sold in grocery stores.

1 Mix together the cabbage, carrots, scallions, yogurt, mustard, and lemon juice in a serving bowl. Season the slaw with black pepper to taste.

mini cheese & chive tarts

Makes 6

Preparation time 20 minutes, plus chilling

Cooking time 25–30 minutes

dairy-free spread, for greasing

1 sheet store-bought, ready-to-bake dairy-free puff pastry

flour, for dusting

⅔ cup unsweetened dairy-free milk

3 tablespoons dairy-free cream

3 eggs

1 heaping teaspoon Dijon mustard

3 tablespoons nutritional yeast flakes

2 tablespoons snipped chives

3 cherry tomatoes, halved

These individual tarts are cooked in a jumbo muffin pan, which makes them much easier to make and also means they look really cute.

1 Lightly grease the cups of a 6-cup jumbo muffin pan. Roll out the pastry on a lightly floured work surface and use to line the prepared muffin cups, leaving the pastry edges standing slightly above the pan. Chill the pastry shells for 15 minutes.

2 Whisk together the milk, cream, eggs, and mustard in a small bowl until combined, then stir in the yeast flakes and chives. Pour the mixture into the prepared pastry shells.

3 Place in a preheated oven, at 400°F, for 6–8 minutes, until starting to set, then remove from the oven and place half a tomato on top of each tart. Return to the oven and continue to cook for another 19–22 minutes, until risen and the pastry is cooked through. Let cool in the pan for 5 minutes, then turn out onto a wire rack. Serve warm or cold.

Indian lamb skewers

Serves 4

Preparation time 20 minutes, plus chilling

Cooking time 40 minutes

2 tablespoons sunflower oil

½ large onion, finely chopped

2 large garlic cloves, finely chopped

1 inch piece of fresh ginger root, peeled and finely chopped

1 (14½ oz) can diced tomatoes

1½ cups lamb broth

1 tablespoon tomato paste

2 teaspoons garam masala

1 teaspoon ground coriander

Skewers

½ large onion, cut into wedges

1 large garlic clove, peeled

1 inch piece of fresh ginger root, peeled

2 teaspoons garam masala

1 cup fresh bread crumbs

12 oz ground lamb

1 tablespoon tomato paste

salt and black pepper

To serve

cooked brown long-grain rice

¼ cup dairy-free yogurt, preferably unsweetened

handful of fresh cilantro, chopped

1 red chile, seeded and finely chopped (optional)

These lightly spiced lamb meatballs are cooked in a mild curry sauce. If your children like slightly hot food, you could add a few red pepper flakes to spice it up a little more.

1 Make the skewers. Put the onion, garlic, and ginger into a food processor or blender and process to a coarse paste. Add the garam masala, bread crumbs, lamb, and tomato paste, season with salt and black pepper, and process briefly until combined. Shape the lamb mixture into 20 small walnut-size balls, cover, and chill for about 30 minutes.

2 Heat half the oil in a large saucepan, add the lamb skewers, in 2 batches, and cook for 5 minutes, until golden all over. Remove from the pan and set aside.

3 Heat the remaining oil in the pan, add the onion, and cook for 5 minutes, until softened, then add the garlic and ginger and cook for another 1 minute. Add the tomatoes, broth, and tomato paste and bring to a boil. Reduce the heat and simmer for 5 minutes. Using an immersion blender, puree the sauce until smooth, then stir in the garam masala and ground coriander.

4 Return the browned lamb skewers to the pan and simmer, partly covered, for 20 minutes, stirring occasionally, until the sauce has reduced and thickened.

5 Serve the skewers with rice, topped with yogurt, cilantro, and chile, if desired.

tandoori roasted chicken

Serves 4

**Preparation time 15 minutes,
plus marinating and resting**

Cooking time 1 hour 20 minutes

1 (3 lb) chicken

1 cup water

1 recipe quantity Dairy-Free Raita
(*see* page 136), to serve

Tandoori marinade

3 tablespoons tandoori spice mix

2 teaspoons turmeric

3 garlic cloves, crushed

1 inch piece of unpeeled fresh ginger
root, grated

juice of 1 lime

⅔ cup dairy-free yogurt, preferably
unsweetened

salt and black pepper

A combination of dairy-free yogurt and spices makes a fantastic marinade for chicken and keeps it wonderfully moist while roasting. The chicken is just as good served warm with roasted potatoes as it is cold with a salad and garlic mayonnaise.

1 Mix together all the marinade ingredients in a nonreactive bowl and season. Put the chicken on a plate and spoon the marinade over it. Wearing a pair of rubber gloves, rub the marinade into the chicken until it is thoroughly coated all over. Cover the chicken with a double layer of plastic wrap and let marinate in the refrigerator for at least 3 hours, or preferably overnight.

2 Place the chicken on a rack above a roasting pan and pour the measured water into the pan (this will help to keep the chicken moist and can be used as a base for a gravy). Roast in a preheated oven, at 400°F, for about 1 hour 20 minutes, basting occasionally, until cooked through and the juices run clear when the thickest part of the thigh is pierced with the tip of a sharp knife. Remove the chicken from the oven, cover with a double layer of aluminum foil, and let rest for 20 minutes. Carve into slices and serve with the Dairy-Free Raita.

desserts

vanilla coconut balls

Serves 4

Preparation time 10 minutes,
  plus cooling and freezing

Cooking time 2 minutes

½ cup flaked unsweetened dried coconut

4 scoops of dairy-free vanilla ice cream

2½ cups bite-size fresh pineapple pieces,
  or a combination of pineapple, peach,
  or mango pieces

To decorate (optional)

maple syrup or honey

toasted slivered almonds

This simple dessert takes store-bought
dairy-free vanilla ice cream to a new level.

1 Put the coconut into a large, dry skillet and toast for 2 minutes,
tossing the pan occasionally, until golden. Transfer the coconut
onto a plate and let cool.

2 Take a scoop of ice cream and roll it in the toasted coconut
until evenly coated. Repeat with the remaining ice cream and
coconut. Place the ice cream balls in the freezer for 10 minutes,
until slightly firm.

3 Spoon the fruit into 4 tall glasses and place a ball of coconut-
coated ice cream on top. Drizzle each with maple syrup or
honey and sprinkle with a few slivered almonds, if desired.

maple caramel fro-yo

Serves 6

**Preparation time 10 minutes,
plus freezing**

2 bananas, chopped

½ cup coconut drinking milk
(*see* page 135 for homemade)

½ cup dairy-free coconut yogurt

2 teaspoons vanilla extract

2 tablespoons maple syrup or honey

½ quantity Dairy-Free Caramel Sauce
(*see* page 141)

1 Put all the ingredients except the caramel sauce into a food processor or blender and blend together until smooth and creamy. Spoon into a freezer-proof container with a lid and freeze for 3 hours or until ice crystals start to form.

2 Remove from the freezer and beat well to break up the ice crystals, then gently stir in the caramel sauce to form a swirly pattern. Return to the freezer for about 3 hours, until frozen.

3 Remove the fro-yo from the freezer to soften about 20 minutes before serving.

Hints and tips

You only need half the recipe quantity of the caramel sauce to swirl into the frozen yogurt; the rest will keep in the refrigerator for up to 5 days. The sauce is delicious spooned over fruit or dairy-free ice cream or yogurt, or used in the Raspberry & Caramel Trifles (*see* page 128).

mango kulfi

Serves 4

Preparation time 15 minutes,
 plus freezing

Cooking time 5 minutes

olive oil, for greasing

1¾ cups unsweetened almond milk
 (*see* page 134 for homemade)
 or other dairy-free milk

2 slices of white bread, crusts removed,
 torn into bite-size pieces

1 large ripe mango, halved, pitted,
 and sliced

2 tablespoons honey

1 teaspoon vanilla extract

To decorate (optional)

freshly grated nutmeg

2 tablespoons shelled pistachio nuts,
 toasted and chopped

1 Lightly grease four ⅔ cup metal dessert molds with oil. Pour the almond milk into a medium saucepan and bring almost to a boil, then add the bread and stir until it starts to break down.

2 Pour the mixture into a food processor or blender, add the mango, honey, and vanilla extract, and blend until smooth and creamy. Pour the mixture into the prepared molds and freeze for about 3 hours, until firm.

3 Remove from the freezer to soften about 20 minutes before serving. Turn the kulfi upside down and pour a little hot water over the bottom of each mold to release the kulfi. Place on serving plates, then grate over a little nutmeg and sprinkle with toasted pistachios, if desired.

mixed berry whips

Serves 4

Preparation time 15 minutes

1 cup frozen mixed berries, such as rasberries, hulled strawberries, and blueberries, defrosted

125 ml (4 fl oz) dairy-free yogurt

¼ cup dairy-free cream cheese

1 extra-large egg white

1 tablespoon superfine or granulated sugar

handful of mixed berries, to decorate

Having a bag or or two of frozen fruit in the freezer is always a useful backup for making whips, ice creams, and smoothies or to serve simply with dairy-free cream.

1 Put the fruit, yogurt, and cream cheese in a food processor or blender and blend together.

2 Whisk the egg white in a large, grease-free bowl until it holds its shape. Gradually add the sugar, whisking well between each addition, until the mixture is stiff and glossy, then fold into the fruit mixture, using a metal spoon.

3 Spoon the whip into 4 small glasses and chill the desserts until ready to serve. Decorate with mixed berries.

yummy hot nut chocolate

Serves 1

Preparation time 5 minutes

Cooking time 5 minutes

1¼ cups Rich Nut Milk (*see* page 134) or other unsweetened nut milk

2 squares of dairy-free semsiweet chocolate, broken into small pieces

¼ teaspoon ground cinnamon, plus extra to serve

maple syrup, honey, or light brown sugar, to taste

fruit, for dunking (optional)

Rich and chocolaty, this is real hot chocolate—the powdered stuff just can't compare to it. It makes a treat of a beverage.

1 Heat the milk and chocolate in a small saucepan over low heat, stirring, until the chocolate melts. Add the cinnamon and heat through until warm and thick.

2 Add syrup, honey, or sugar to taste, then pour into a mug and sprinkle with extra cinnamon. Serve with fresh fruit for dunking, if desired.

fruity ice pops

Makes 6–8

Preparation time 15 minutes, plus cooling and freezing

Cooking time 5 minutes

3 ripe nectarines, halved, pitted, and chopped

2 tablespoons confectioners' sugar, plus extra to taste

1 tablespoon water

1 cup frozen pitted dark cherries

½ quantity Dairy-Free Custard (*see* page 139 for homemade)

1 Put the nectarines into a saucepan with the sugar and measured water, then slowly bring almost to a boil. Reduce the heat and simmer for about 5 minutes, stirring occasionally, until softened. Let cool.

2 Put the nectarines in a food processor or blender, add the cherries and custard, and blend until smooth and creamy. Add a little extra confectioners' sugar, if desired.

3 Spoon the fruit mixture into 6–8 ice cream molds, depending on their size, and freeze until firm.

strawberry soufflé omelet

Serves 2

Preparation time 15 minutes

Cooking time 5 minutes

2 eggs, separated

2 teaspoons superfine or granulated sugar

½ teaspoon vanilla extract

1 teaspoon dairy-free spread or coconut oil

1 cup hulled and halved strawberries

large handful of blueberries

confectioners' sugar, for dusting

Cashew Cream (*see* page 140), Coconut Vanilla Cream (*see* page 141), or dairy-free yogurt, to serve

It may be surprising to learn that omelets can be sweet as well as savory. This one is light as a cloud and topped with plenty of fresh strawberries and blueberries.

1 Whisk the egg whites in a large, grease-free bowl until they hold their shape. Gradually add the sugar, whisking well between each addition, until the mixture is stiff and glossy. Whisk in the vanilla extract. Beat the egg yolks, then gently fold them in.

2 Melt the spread or coconut oil in a medium ovenproof skillet and swirl it to around to coat the bottom. Pour the frothy egg mixture into the pan and gently spread it out with a spatula, leaving a few peaks and troughs. Cook over medium-low heat for 2–3 minutes, until the bottom is set and light golden. Place under a preheated hot broiler and lightly cook the top until just set.

3 Slide the omelet onto a serving plate and top with the strawberries and blueberries and a dusting of confectioners' sugar. Divide the omelet in 2, then serve with spoonfuls of Cashew Cream, Coconut Vanilla Cream, or yogurt.

melon slush

Serves 4–6

**Preparation time 15 minutes,
plus freezing**

¼ ripe watermelon or 1 small honeydew
melon or canteloupe

juice of 2 limes

3 tablespoons confectioners' sugar,
plus extra to taste

strips of lime zest, to decorate (optional)

This fresh fruit slush is super-refreshing on
a hot summer's day.

1 Quarter the melon and remove the seeds. Scoop out the flesh
into a food processor or blender and blend to a coarse puree.

2 Pour into a freezer-proof container with a lid. Stir in the lime
juice and sugar, adding extra, if desired. Freeze for 2 hours.

3 Remove from the freezer and break up the ice crystals, using
a fork. Return to the freezer for 2 hours or until frozen.

4 Remove from the freezer to soften about 20 minutes before
serving. Using a fork, scrape the top of the frozen melon
into loose crystals, then spoon the slush into glasses. Serve
decorated with a few strips of lime zest, if desired.

custards with rhubarb

Serves 4

Preparation time 15 minutes,
  plus steeping

Cooking time 30 minutes

dairy-free spread, for greasing

1¼ cups unsweetened dairy-free milk

1 cup oat cream or other dairy-free cream

1 cinnamon stick

3 extra-large eggs, lightly beaten

¼ cup superfine or granulated sugar

1 teaspoon vanilla extract

Rhubarb

4 rhubarb stalks, sliced

2 tablespoons superfine or granulated
  sugar

finely grated zest and juice of ½ orange

This classic combination can't be beaten! You may notice that many of the dessert recipes in this book feature vanilla extract and/or spices. There are two good reasons for this: first, they taste delicious; and, second, it means you don't need to use so much sugar—a double bonus.

1 Lightly grease four ⅔ cup dessert molds or large ramekins.

2 Put the milk, cream, and cinnamon stick in a small saucepan and heat to almost boiling point, stirring occasionally. Remove the pan from the heat and let steep for 10 minutes.

3 Meanwhile, whisk together the eggs and sugar in a bowl until pale and creamy.

4 When steeped, briefly reheat the milk, then strain into the egg mixture, discarding the cinnamon, and stir in the vanilla extract.

5 Pour the custard into the prepared dessert molds and put them into a baking pan. Pour enough just-boiled water into the pan to come two-thirds of the way up the mold sides. Carefully place in a preheated oven, at 350°F, for 25 minutes or until the custards have set but are still slightly wobbly. Meanwhile, put the rhubarb, sugar, and orange zest and juice into a saucepan and heat gently for 8–10 minutes, until tender.

6 Remove the custards from the oven and let cool slightly, then run a knife around the inside edge of each mold and turn out into serving bowls. Serve with the rhubarb.

chocolate & avocado puddings

Serves 4

Preparation time 15 minutes,
plus soaking and chilling

3 dried dates, quartered

⅓ cup just-boiled water

1 large avocado, halved, pitted,
and peeled

⅓ cup good-quality cocoa powder

1 teaspoon vanilla extract

4 teaspoons maple syrup or honey

½ cup unsweetened almond milk
(*see* page 134 for homemade)
or other dairy-free milk

1 teaspoon coconut oil, melted

¼ cup Cashew Cream (*see* page 140)
or other dairy-free cream

favorite fruit, to serve

No one will catch on that these indulgent little chocolate puddings contain avocado—best keep it a secret.

1 Put the dates in a heatproof bowl, cover with the measured water, and let soak for 30 minutes, until softened.

2 Put the dates and soaking water into a food processor or blender, add the avocado, cocoa powder, vanilla extract, maple syrup, milk, and coconut oil and blend until smooth and creamy.

3 Spoon the mixture into 4 small glasses or ramekins and chill for 30 minutes. Top each with the cashew cream and serve with your favorite fruit.

apple syrup cakes

Serves 4

Preparation time 15 minutes

Cooking time 30–35 minutes

⅓ cup dairy-free spread, plus extra
  for greasing

⅓ cup superfine or granulated sugar

¾ cup all-purpose flour

1¼ teaspoons baking powder

1 teaspoon vanilla extract

2 eggs, lightly beaten

3 tablespoons unsweetened
  dairy-free milk

1 unpeeled crisp, sweet apple, grated

4 heaping teaspoons light corn syrup

1 quantity warm Dairy-Free Custard
  (*see* page 139), to serve

1 Lightly grease four ⅔ cup fluted or plain metal dessert molds.

2 Put the spread, sugar, flour, baking powder, vanilla extract, eggs, and milk in a food processor or blender and blend together for 2 minutes, until smooth and creamy. Alternatively, place in a bowl and beat together using a handheld electric mixer. Fold in the apple.

3 Spoon 1 heaping teaspoon of the syrup into each prepared mold, then top with the apple mixture. Transfer the molds to a baking pan and bake in a preheated oven, at 350°F, for 30–35 minutes, until risen and golden. Let cool for a few minutes, then run a knife around the inside edge of each mold and turn out onto serving plates. Serve with warm custard.

apple & blueberry crisp

Serves 4–6

Preparation time 15 minutes

Cooking time 40 minutes

2 Granny Smith apples, peeled, cored, and cut into bite-size pieces

1/3 cup superfine or granulated sugar

2 tablespoons water

3 handfuls of blueberries or blackberries

dairy-free vanilla ice cream or Dairy-Free Custard (see page 139), to serve

Topping

1/3 cup all-purpose flour

1/4 cup firmly packed light brown sugar

1/2 cup rolled oats

1/3 cup ground almonds (almond meal)

1/2 teaspoon ground cinnamon

1/4 cup pecans, coarsely chopped

1/3 cup coconut oil

This variation on the typical apple crisp has a lightly spiced crunchy oat, nut, and coconut oil topping.

1 Put the apples, superfine or granulated sugar, and measured water into a saucepan, cover, and cook for 6–8 minutes, until the apples start to break down. Spoon into a 1¼ quart ovenproof dish and stir in the blueberries or blackberries.

2 Mix together all of the topping ingredients, except the coconut oil, in a bowl. Heat the coconut oil gently in a small saucepan, then let cool slightly. Pour into the dry ingredients, then stir until combined and the mixture comes together in small clumps.

3 Spoon the topping onto the fruit and place in a preheated oven, at 350°F, for 30 minutes or until slightly crisp and golden on top. Serve with dairy-free vanilla ice cream or custard.

fruit bun pudding

Serves 6

Preparation time 15 minutes,
 plus standing

Cooking time 40–45 minutes

6 dairy-free hot cross buns or other
 fruit rolls, halved

dairy-free spread, for spreading

⅔ cup dairy-free cream

1¼ cups unsweetened dairy-free milk

1 teaspoon vanilla extract

1 teaspoon allspice

3 eggs

¼ cup superfine or granulated sugar,
 plus extra for sprinkling

This dairy-free version of bread-and-butter pudding is made with hot cross buns or fruit rolls. You could also add a handful of chopped dried apricots to the dessert and sprinkle pecans over the top.

1 Spread the hot cross buns with spread, then arrange in 2 layers, slightly overlapping and spread side up, in a 1¼ quart ovenproof dish.

2 Put the cream, milk, vanilla extract, and allspice into a saucepan and bring almost to a boil. Meanwhile, whisk together the eggs and superfine or granulated sugar in a heatproof bowl. Pour in the cream mixture, whisking continuously, until combined.

3 Pour the custard mixture over the hot cross buns, pressing them down into the liquid. Let stand for 10 minutes, then sprinkle over a little extra sugar.

4 Place the dish in a baking pan and pour in enough just-boiled water to come halfway up the sides. Carefully place in a preheated oven, at 350°F, and cook for 35–40 minutes, until set and crisp and golden on top.

raspberry popovers

Makes 6

Preparation time 10 minutes,
plus standing

Cooking time 25 minutes

½ cup all-purpose flour

pinch of salt

½ cup unsweetened almond milk
(*see* page 134 for homemade) or
other dairy-free milk

1 extra-large egg, lightly beaten

3 teaspoons sunflower oil

To serve

fresh raspberries

maple syrup or honey

Cashew Cream (*see* page 140) or
Coconut Vanilla Cream (*see* page 141)

The simplest way to describe these would
be a sweet version of the classic popovers
served with roast beef—and they are just
yummy. You need to get the oil really hot
before adding the batter so that they rise
and become light and fluffy inside.

1 Sift the flour, baking powder, and salt into a large bowl and
make a well in the center. Whisk together the milk and egg
in a small bowl, then gradually pour into the dry ingredients,
whisking continuously to form a smooth batter. Transfer the
batter to a small bowl and let stand for 20 minutes.

2 Divide the oil among a 6-cup muffin pan. Heat in a preheated
oven, at 425°F, for 6 minutes, until hot. Carefully remove the
pan from the oven and pour in the batter. Return to the oven
and cook for 17–20 minutes, until risen and golden.

3 Sprinkle raspberries over each popover, then drizzle with syrup
or honey and serve with good spoonfuls of dairy-free cream.

coconut rice pudding

Serves 4

Preparation time 10 minutes

Cooking time 30 minutes

⅔ cup short-grain brown rice

2 cups coconut drinking milk (*see* page 135 for homemade), plus extra if needed

¼ cup superfine or granulated sugar

½ teaspoon ground cinnamon or crushed cardamom seeds

1 teaspoon vanilla extract

To serve

sliced or chopped fresh or dried fruit, such as mango, banana, pear, dried apricots, dates, or raisins

handful of pecans, toasted and coarsely chopped

Rice pudding, if made in the traditional way, takes a while to bake. This speedy version uses short-grain brown rice, but if you can't find it you could use short-grain white rice.

1 Cook the rice according to the package directions until tender, then drain, if necessary, and return the rice to the pan.

2 Pour the milk into the pan and heat over medium-low heat for 10 minutes, stirring continuously and adding a little extra milk if the mixture looks too dry. Stir in the sugar, cinnamon or cardamom, and vanilla extract and cook for another 5 minutes, until thick and creamy.

3 Spoon the pudding into 4 bowls and serve topped with fruit and chopped pecans.

banana melts

Serves 4

Preparation time 10 minutes

4 bananas, sliced

½ cup dairy-free cream cheese

½ cup dairy-free yogurt, preferably unsweetened

1 teaspoon vanilla extract

4 teaspoons packed light brown sugar

Perfect for a weekday dessert, this is quick and easy to make.

1 Divide the bananas among 4 serving glasses or bowls.

2 Put the cream cheese, yogurt, and vanilla extract into a bowl and beat together until smooth, then spoon it over the bananas.

3 Sprinkle 1 teaspoon of the sugar over each serving and wait for a few minutes for it to melt before serving.

cherry cheesecake brûlées

Serves 4

Preparation time 15 minutes, plus cooling

Cooking time 5 minutes

1 heaping teaspoon cornstarch

2 teaspoons water

1 (10 oz) package frozen pitted
   dark cherries

4 dairy-free graham crackers, crushed

1½ cup dairy-free cream cheese

½ cup dairy-free coconut yogurt
   or other thick dairy-free yogurt

2 heaping teaspoons Demerara
   or other raw sugar

A cross between a cheesecake and a crème brûlée, these individual desserts need to be made in advance to allow time for chilling.

1 Mix the cornstarch and measured water to a paste in a cup. Put the cherries into a saucepan with a splash of water and heat until defrosted. Stir in the cornstarch paste and cook, stirring, for 2 minutes, until thickened. Let cool.

2 Divide the crushed cookies among 4 ramekins and top with the cherry mixture.

3 Put the cream cheese and yogurt into a bowl and beat together until smooth and creamy, then spoon the mixture over the cherries in an even layer. Sprinkle the sugar over the ramekins and mist the tops with a splash of water (this helps the sugar to caramelize).

4 Transfer the ramekins to a broiler pan and place under a preheated hot broiler for 2–3 minutes or until the sugar melts and starts to caramelize (keep an eye on them because the sugar can burn easily). Let cool, or chill, before serving.

treats &
special occasions

lemon & almond drizzle

Serves 12

Preparation time 15 minutes, plus cooling

Cooking time 45–50 minutes

¾ cup dairy-free spread, plus extra
 for greasing

¾ cup plus 2 tablespoons superfine
 or granulated sugar

3 eggs

⅓ cups all-purpose flour

1¼ teaspoons baking powder

finely grated zest of 2 lemons

1 teaspoon vanilla extract

½ cup ground almonds (almond meal)

3 tablespoons lemon juice

Lemon icing

⅓ cup confectioners' sugar

1½–2 tablespoons lemon juice

This moist, lemony cake is made in a loaf pan, but it also looks pretty baked in mini individual loaf pans or paper cupcake liners.

1 Lightly grease and line the bottom of an 8½ x 4½ x 2½ inch loaf pan.

2 Beat together the spread and superfine or granulated sugar in a large bowl until pale and fluffy. Add the eggs, one at a time, beating well between each addition and adding a spoonful of flour if the mixture starts to curdle. Stir in the lemon zest and vanilla extract. Sift in the flour, baking powder, and ground almonds, then fold in the lemon juice.

3 Spoon the batter into the prepared loaf pan and smooth the top with the back of the spoon. Cook in a preheated oven, at 350°F, for 45–50 minutes, until a toothpick inserted into the center comes out clean. Let cool in the pan for 5 minutes, then turn out onto a wire rack, remove the parchment paper, and let cool.

4 Make the icing. Sift the confectioners' sugar into a bowl and stir in enough lemon juice to form a soft but not runny icing. Drizzle the icing over the top of the cooled cake and let set.

merry berry phyllo tarts

Makes 8

Preparation time 15 minutes, plus cooling

Cooking time 20 minutes

¼ cup coconut oil, melted

8 sheets of phyllo pastry (about
  12 x 7 inches each)

1 quantity Coconut Vanilla Cream
  (*see* page 141)

2 cups mixed berries, such as blueberries,
  hulled strawberries, and raspberries

2 teaspoons confectioners' sugar,
  for dusting

1 Grease 8 cups of a 12-cup muffin pan with a little of the melted coconut oil.

2 Cut each sheet of phyllo into three 4 inch squares to make 24 squares in total; discard the pastry scraps.

3 Carefully press a square of phyllo into each prepared cup in the muffin pan and lightly brush with the melted coconut oil. Place a second sheet of phyllo diagonally on top, brush with more coconut oil, then place a final sheet of phyllo in each cup to make 8 baskets with a star-shape top.

4 Cook in a preheated oven, at 350°F, for about 20 minutes or until golden and crisp. Transfer to a wire rack to cool.

5 Spoon the coconut vanilla cream into the phyllo cups and top with the berries. Dust with confectioners' sugar before serving.

chocolate beet brownies

Makes 12

Preparation time 15 minutes, plus cooling

Cooking time 25–30 minutes

⅔ cup sunflower oil, plus extra
   for greasing

4 oz dairy-free semisweet chocolate,
   broken into pieces

3 eggs

1 cup superfine or granulated sugar

¾ cup all-purpose flour

½ cup unsweetened cocoa powder,
   plus extra to decorate

½ cup ground almonds (almond meal)

1¾ teaspoons baking powder

4 cooked beets, patted dry and shredded

1 teaspoon vanilla extract

1 Grease and line the bottom of an 8 inch square cake pan.

2 Melt the chocolate in a bowl set over a saucepan of gently simmering water, making sure the bottom of the bowl doesn't touch the water, then let cool slightly.

3 Meanwhile, whisk together the eggs and sugar in a large bowl until pale and fluffy. Gradually beat in the oil, flour, cocoa powder, almonds, baking powder, beets, and vanilla extract, then add the melted chocolate.

4 Pour the batter into the prepared pan and cook in a preheated oven, at 350°F, for 20–25 minutes, until risen and just cooked; it should still be slightly squashy in the middle. Let cool in the pan for 5 minutes, then turn out onto a wire rack and let cool. Remove the parchment paper and decorate with a light dusting of cocoa powder. Cut into 12 squares before serving.

fruit 'n' nut cookies

Makes 12

Preparation time 15 minutes, plus cooling

Cooking time 18 minutes

½ cup dried apricots

¾ cup all-purpose flour

¾ cup rolled oats

½ cup chopped hazelnuts

½ cup dairy-free spread or coconut oil

⅓ cup firmly packed light brown sugar

2 tablespoons light corn syrup

1 Line a baking sheet with nonstick parchment paper. Cut the apricots into small pieces. Put the flour, oats, hazelnuts, and apricot pieces into a bowl and stir until combined.

2 Put the spread or oil, sugar, and syrup into a small saucepan and heat gently, stirring occasionally, until melted. Pour into the dry ingredients and stir to form a soft, chunky dough.

3 Place 12 tablespoonfuls of dough on the prepared baking sheet, spaced well apart, and flatten the tops slightly. Bake in a preheated oven, at 350°F, for 15 minutes or until light golden. Transfer to a wire rack to cool until crisp.

peanut butter cookies

Makes 10

Preparation time 15 minutes

Cooking time 17–20 minutes

3 oz dairy-free semisweet chocolate

⅓ cup unsalted roasted peanuts

3 tablespoons peanut butter

¼ cup dairy-free spread

½ cup firmly packed light brown sugar

1 egg, lightly beaten

¾ cup all-purpose flour

½ teaspoon baking powder

pinch of salt

1 Line a baking sheet with nonstick parchment paper. Break the chocolate into chunks and coarsely chop the roasted peanuts.

2 Beat together the peanut butter, spread, and sugar in a large bowl until light and creamy. Beat in the egg, adding a spoonful of the flour if the mixture starts to curdle. Fold in the flour, baking powder, and salt, then the chocolate pieces and peanuts.

3 Spoon 10 tablespoonfuls of the dough onto the prepared baking sheet and flatten the tops slightly. Place in a preheated oven, at 350°F, for 17–20 minutes, until golden but still slightly soft and gooey in the centers. Transfer to a wire rack to cool.

banana muffins with cinnamon frosting

Makes 10

Preparation time 20 minutes, plus cooling and chilling

Cooking time 20–25 minutes

1¾ cups plus 1 tablespoon all-purpose flour

1½ teaspoons baking powder

¾ cup firmly packed light brown sugar

2 extra-large eggs

¼ cup unsweetened dairy-free milk

½ cup dairy-free spread or coconut oil, melted and cooled

2 large ripe bananas, mashed

Cinnamon frosting

½ cup dairy-free cream cheese

⅔ cup confectioners' sugar, plus extra to taste

1 teaspoon vanilla extract

1 teaspoon ground cinnamon

1 Line 10 cups of a 12-hole muffin pan with paper muffin cups.

2 Sift the flour, baking powder, and brown sugar into a large bowl. Stir until combined, then make a well in the center. Beat together the eggs, milk, and melted spread or oil in a small bowl, then pour into the dry ingredients and add the bananas. Using a wooden spoon, gently stir together until just combined.

3 Spoon the batter into the muffin cups and cook in a preheated oven, at 375°F, for 20–25 minutes or until risen. Transfer to a wire rack to cool.

4 Meanwhile, make the cinnamon frosting. Put the cream cheese, confectioners' sugar, vanilla extract, and cinnamon in a bowl and beat together until smooth, thick, and creamy, adding a little extra confectioners' sugar to taste, if desired, then chill until firm. Decorate each muffin with a spoonful of the frosting.

Hints and tips
The secret to light, moist muffins is to not overmix the cake batter; it doesn't matter if the ingredients aren't thoroughly combined.

mini strawberry vanilla cheesecakes

Makes 4–6

Preparation time 20 minutes, plus cooling and chilling

Cooking time 30 minutes

3 tablespoons dairy-free spread

½ cup crushed dairy-free graham crackers or vanilla or butter cookies

2½ tablespoons ground almonds (almond meal)

2 cups hulled and halved strawberries

2 teaspoons confectioners' sugar

Filling

½ cup dairy-free yogurt, preferably unsweetened

¾ cup dairy-free cream cheese

2 tablespoons dairy-free cream

2 egg yolks, beaten

2 tablespoons maple syrup or honey

1 teaspoon vanilla extract

juice of ½ lemon

1½ teaspoons cornstarch

A deep muffin pan is the perfect container for these individual cheesecakes, which are just the perfect size for children.

1 Line four 1 cup mini cheesecake pans with parchment paper. Alternatively, line 6 cups of a muffin pan with parchment paper by cutting 2 strips and pressing them into the muffin cups, laying one perpendicular to the other to form a cross shape.

2 Melt the spread in a small saucepan, then stir in the crushed cookies and ground almonds. Divide the mixture evenly among the prepared cheesecake pans and press down to make firm, even crusts. Cook in a preheated oven, at 350°F, for 10 minutes, until just crisp.

3 Meanwhile, beat together all the filling ingredients in a bowl until smooth and creamy. Spoon the mixture over the cookie crusts and level the tops, then return to the oven for another 17–20 minutes or until firm and just set. Let cool in the pans, then chill for at least 30 minutes.

4 Put the strawberries into a bowl and sprinkle with the confectioners' sugar. Stir together, then let stand until the juices start to run.

5 When ready to serve, carefully remove the cheesecakes from the pans onto serving plates. Spoon the strawberries and any juice on top of the cheesecakes.

strawberries & cream birthday cake

Serves 8–10

Preparation time 20 minutes, plus cooling and chilling

Cooking time 35–45 minutes

3¼ cups all-purpose flour, plus extra for dusting

1½ tablespoons baking powder

½ teaspoon baking soda

1¼ cups superfine or granulated sugar

½ cup sunflower oil

1⅔ cups unsweetened almond milk (*see* page 134 for homemade) or other dairy-free milk

3 tablespoons light corn syrup

2 teaspoons vanilla extract

¼ cup strawberry preserves

Buttercream

¾ cup dairy-free spread, plus extra for greasing

1⅓ cups confectioners' sugar, sifted, plus extra to decorate

1 teaspoon vanilla extract

To decorate

2 handfuls of dairy-free chocolate disks

1 cup hulled and halved or quartered (depending on size) strawberries

This simple celebration cake is topped with dairy-free buttercream and chocolate disks, along with fresh strawberries.

1 Grease and flour the sides of two 9 inch loose-bottom cake pans, then line the bottoms with parchment paper.

2 Sift the flour, baking powder, baking soda, and sugar into a large bowl, then stir together. Whisk together the oil, milk, syrup, and vanilla extract in a small bowl, then pour into the dry ingredients and whisk for 2 minutes, until thick and creamy.

3 Spoon the batter into the prepared cake pans and bake in a preheated oven, at 350°F, for 35–45 minutes, until risen and cooked through. Let cool in the pans for 10 minutes, then turn out onto a wire rack, remove the parchment paper, and let cool completely.

4 Meanwhile, make the buttercream. Beat together all the ingredients in a bowl until thick and creamy, then chill until firm.

5 Spread the preserves evenly over 1 cake and top with two-thirds of the buttercream. Top with the remaining cake and spread the remaining buttercream over the top. Decorate the top edge of the cake with chocolate disks and pile the strawberries in the center. Dust with extra confectioners' sugar before serving.

easy chocolate cherry cake

Serves 12

Preparation time 15 minutes, plus cooling and chilling

Cooking time 45–50 minutes

⅓ cup plus 1 teaspoon sunflower oil, plus extra for greasing

1¾ cups all-purpose flour

1 cup plus 2 tablespoons superfine or granulated sugar

1 teaspoon baking soda

½ teaspoon salt

3 tablespoons good-quality unsweetened cocoa powder

1 teaspoon vanilla extract

1 tablespoon distilled white vinegar

1 cup water

⅔ cup dried cherries

Chocolate frosting

½ cup dairy-free cream cheese

⅓ cup confectioners' sugar, sifted

1 teaspoon unsweetened cocoa powder

1 teaspoon vanilla extract

Egg-free, this is one of the easiest cakes to make and tastes delicious, too.

1 Lightly grease and line an 8½ x 4½ x 2½ inch loaf pan.

2 Sift the flour, superfine or granulated sugar, baking soda, salt, and cocoa powder into a large bowl, then stir until combined. In a separate bowl, mix together the oil, vanilla extract, vinegar, and measured water. Pour into the dry ingredients, add the cherries, and stir with a wooden spoon until combined.

3 Pour the batter into the prepared pan and bake in a preheated oven, at 350°F, for 45–50 minutes, until risen and a toothpick inserted into the center comes out clean. Let cool in the pan for 5 minutes, then turn out onto a wire rack, remove the parchment paper, and let cool completely.

4 Put all the frosting ingredients into a bowl and beat together until smooth and creamy. Chill for 30 minutes, until firm, then spoon the frosting over the cake before serving.

raspberry & caramel trifles

Serves 6

Preparation time 20 minutes, plus cooling and chilling

Cooking time 35 minutes

2½ cups frozen raspberries, defrosted

1½ quantities (2 cups) Dairy-Free Custard (*see* page 139), cooled

½ quantity Coconut Vanilla Cream (*see* page 141) or 2 quantities Cashew Cream (*see* page 140)

½ quantity Dairy-Free Caramel Sauce (*see* page 141) or 1 oz dairy-free semisweet chocolate, grated

Cake

⅔ cup dairy-free spread, plus extra for greasing

¾ cup superfine or granulated sugar

1 teaspoon vanilla extract

1¼ cups all-purpose flour

1¾ teaspoons baking powder

1 extra-large egg, lightly beaten

¼ cup unsweetened dairy-free milk

This is a conglomeration of a few recipes in this book, which all come together to make a treat of a dessert—just the thing for a special occasion. The trifle can also be made in a single large serving bowl.

1 Grease and line a 9 inch loose-bottom cake pan.

2 Beat together all the cake ingredients in a large bowl for 2 minutes, until pale and creamy. Spoon the batter into the prepared pan and bake in a preheated oven, at 350°F, for 35 minutes or until risen and cooked through. Let cool in the pan for 5 minutes, then turn out onto a wire rack, remove the parchment paper, and let cool completely.

3 Break the cake into pieces and divide among 6 individual dessert glasses. Put the raspberries in a separate bowl and lightly crush with the back of a fork. Spoon them over the cake pieces, then divide the custard among the glasses, spreading it evenly over the top of the crushed raspberries. Spoon the cream on top, then drizzle with the caramel sauce or sprinkle with the grated chocolate. Chill for 30 minutes before serving.

peaches & cream meringues

Makes 6

Preparation time 15 minutes, plus cooling

Cooking time 30 minutes

3 egg whites

1 teaspoon cornstarch

¾ cup superfine sugar

1 quantity Coconut Vanilla Cream
  (*see* page 141)

3 ripe peaches, halved, pitted and sliced

maple syrup or honey, for drizzling

Make sure the peaches are ripe and juicy when making this pretty summery dessert. In place of the peaches, you could use nectarines, strawberries, raspberries, or cherries.

1 Line a large baking sheet with nonstick parchment paper and draw six 3½ inch circles onto the paper.

2 Using a handheld electric mixer on a low speed, whisk the egg whites in a large, grease-free bowl for about 2 minutes, until foamy, then increase the speed to medium and continue to whisk for 1 minute. Increase the speed to high and whisk until stiff peaks form and the mixture is light and fluffy.

3 Still on a high speed, whisk in the cornstarch and then the sugar, a tablespoon at a time, until the mixture looks stiff and glossy. (Adding the sugar slowly prevents the meringue from weeping when cooked.)

4 Spoon the meringue onto the circles on the parchment paper, then make a slight crater in the center of each one with the back of a spoon. Bake in a preheated oven, at 300°F, for 30 minutes or until the outsides of the meringues are crisp and the centers are slightly soft. Turn off the oven and let the meringues stand in the oven until cold.

5 Place a large dollop of the coconut vanilla cream on each meringue. Arrange the peaches on top, then add a drizzle of maple syrup or honey and serve.

basics

nut milk

Makes about 2 cups

Preparation time 15 minutes,
  plus soaking

1 cup blanched almonds or cashew nuts
2 cups filtered water

Almonds and cashew nuts both make a creamy, nondairy milk. This is an excellent everyday milk for drinking, adding to other recipes, or pouring over cereal.

1 Put the nuts in a bowl and cover with plenty of cold water. Cover with a plate and let soak for 6–8 hours, or overnight.

2 Drain the nuts, discarding the soaking water, and rinse under cold running water. Put into a food processor or blender with the filtered water and blend on a high speed for about 2 minutes or until the nuts are ground into a fine meal and the water is creamy white.

3 Strain the mixture through a nut milk bag or a cheesecloth-lined strainer, reserving the strained milky liquid in a bowl. Gather up the sides of the bag or the cheesecloth and squeeze to extract as much liquid as possible into the bowl. (The nut meal left in the bag can be used to make the nut balls on page 33 or stirred into breakfast muesli, oatmeal, or porridge.)

4 Pour the strained milk into a lidded container and store in the refrigerator for up to 3 days.

Hints and tips
For a thicker Rich Nut Milk, follow the recipe above but reduce the filtered water to 1 cup, and for Nut Cream use ½ cup filtered water—you may need to scrape the nuts down the sides of the food processor or blender and it will take slightly longer to get to a creamy consistency due to the reduced amount of water.

coconut drinking milk

Makes about 1¾ cups

Preparation time 15 minutes, plus overnight soaking

1½ cups dried coconut, preferably unsweetened

1¾ cups filtered water

Excellent for pouring over cereal, you can make this nondairy milk richer and creamier by reducing the amount of filtered water used. After storage, you'll find the cream rises to the surface of the milk—either scrape this off to serve separately or stir until combined again.

1 Put the coconut into a bowl and pour enough cold water over it to cover. Stir well, making sure all the coconut is submerged, cover with a plate, and let soak overnight.

2 Drain the coconut, discarding the soaking water. Put into a food processor or blender with the filtered water and blend on high speed for 2 minutes or until the coconut has turned to a fine meal and the liquid is creamy white.

3 Strain the coconut mixture through a nut milk bag or a cheesecloth-lined strainer, reserving the strained milky liquid in a bowl. Gather up the sides of the bag or the cheesecloth and squeeze to extract as much liquid as possible into the bowl. (The coconut meal left in the bag can be sprinkled over breakfast cereal or muesli or added to cookies and cakes.)

4 Pour the strained milk into a lidded container and store in the refrigerator for up to 3 days.

dairy-free raita

Serves 4

Preparation time 10 minutes

¼ cup dairy-free cream cheese

½ cup unsweetened dairy-free milk

1 tablespoon lemon juice

1 garlic clove, crushed

2 inch piece of cucumber, quartered lengthwise, seeded and diced

salt and black pepper

In place of the usual yogurt, this Indian-style raita is made with a combination of dairy-free cream cheese and milk, then flavored with lemon juice, garlic, and cucumber. A classic accompaniment to Indian curries, a spoonful will help to cool any spicy dish.

1 Mix together the cream cheese, milk, and lemon juice in a serving bowl.

2 Stir in the garlic and cucumber and season with salt and black pepper to taste.

dairy-free tzatziki

Serves 4

Preparation time 10 minutes

½ cup dairy-free yogurt, preferably unsweetened

2 tablespoons dairy-free mayonnaise

1 garlic clove, crushed

1–2 tablespoons lemon juice

2 inch piece of cucumber, quartered lengthwise, seeded and diced

large handful of mint leaves, chopped

salt and black pepper

A dairy-free twist on the Greek classic, this sauce is delicious with broiled or grilled meat and fish as well as roasted vegetables.

1 Mix together the yogurt, mayonnaise, garlic, half the lemon juice, the cucumber, and mint in a serving bowl.

2 Season with salt and black pepper to taste, and add more lemon juice, if desired.

tahini dip

Serves 4

Preparation time 10 minutes

4 oz silken tofu

3 tablespoons light tahini

1 garlic clove, crushed

2 tablespoons extra virgin olive oil

juice of 1 lemon

1–2 tablespoons water

handful of mixed herbs, such as oregano, chives, mint, and parsley, chopped (optional)

salt and black pepper

This creamy dip-cum-sauce makes a nutritious alternative to mayonnaise and is delicious spooned on top of burgers, patties, falafel, and pilafs. It can be made with or without the addition of herbs.

1 Put the tofu, tahini, garlic, oil, lemon juice, and half the measured water into a bowl and blend, using an immersion blender, until smooth and creamy, adding the remaining water, if necessary; the mixture should have the consistency of mayonnaise.

2 Stir in the herbs, if using, and season with salt and black pepper to taste. Store the sauce in an airtight container in the refrigerator for up to 5 days.

dairy-free white sauce

Makes 2½ cups

Preparation time 10 minutes

Cooking time 10 minutes

2½ cups unsweetened dairy-free milk

1 bay leaf

3 tablespoons dairy-free spread

2 heaping tablespoons all-purpose flour

3 tablespoons nutritional yeast flakes

2 teaspoons Dijon mustard

salt and black pepper

A dairy-free white sauce is a useful addition to the cook's repertoire. It can be used as a pouring sauce, flavored with herbs and lemon juice, as a base for a cheesy sauce for pasta and vegetables, or in meat, vegetable, or fish casseroles or pies.

1 Put the milk and bay leaf in a small saucepan and heat gently to simmering point.

2 Melt the spread in a separate saucepan, remove from the heat, and stir in the flour with a wire whisk. Return the pan to low heat and cook the paste for 1–2 minutes, stirring with a wooden spoon until golden.

3 Gradually pour in the warm milk, stirring continuously, then cook for 5–8 minutes or until thickened to a sauce consistency. Stir in the yeast flakes and mustard and season with salt and black pepper to taste.

Hints and tips

To make a dairy-free béchamel sauce, add an onion studded with 6 cloves to the milk and bay leaf in the saucepan and bring to simmering point, then turn off the heat and let steep for 30 minutes. Remove the onion, then reheat the milk briefly and continue as above, omitting the yeast flakes and reducing the mustard to 1 teaspoon.

dairy-free custard

Makes about 1¼ cups

Preparation time 5 minutes

Cooking time 10 minutes

1¼ cups unsweetened dairy-free milk

1 teaspoon vanilla extract

2 extra-large egg yolks

2 tablespoons superfine or
  granulated sugar

1 heaping teaspoon cornstarch

It may be possible to buy nondairy custard
in powdered form, but you still can't beat
homemade fresh custard.

1 Pour the milk and vanilla extract into a saucepan and heat
gently to simmering point.

2 Meanwhile, whisk together the egg yolks, sugar, and cornstarch
in a large heatproof bowl until thickened. Gradually pour the
warmed milk into the egg mixture, whisking continuously.

3 Return the custard to the pan and heat gently over low heat,
stirring with a wooden spoon and making sure you get into the
corners of the pan, until thickened. Pour into a small bowl to serve.

Hints and tips

It's important to heat the milk slowly over low heat
to prevent the egg from scrambling and curdling
in the heat of the milk.

cashew cream

Makes about ½ cup

Preparation time 5 minutes, plus soaking

¾ cup cashew nuts

¼ cup cold water

3 tablespoons dairy-free cream

1 teaspoon vanilla extract

1 tablespoon maple syrup or honey

This sweetened, thick cream is a delicious alternative to whipped cream and can be spooned over fruit, pies, and crisps—it's particularly good on meringues.

1 Put the cashews into a heatproof bowl and cover with just-boiled water. Let soak for 1 hour.

2 Drain the nuts, discarding the soaking liquid. Put into a food processor or blender, add the measured water, and blend until smooth and creamy, scraping down the sides of the small bowl if necessary. Alternatively, blend together using an immersion blender.

3 Stir in the cream, vanilla extract, and maple syrup or honey before serving.

dairy-free caramel sauce

Serves 6

Preparation time 5 minutes

Cooking time 10 minutes

⅓ cup light corn syrup

3 tablespoons packed light brown sugar

3 tablespoons dairy-free spread

½ cup dairy-free cream

This golden sauce can be spooned over dairy-free ice cream or yogurt, or fruit, and will keep in the refrigerator for a short time.

1 Put the corn syrup, sugar, and spread into a small saucepan and bring slowly to a boil. Reduce the heat to low and cook for 5–8 minutes, stirring occasionally, until thickened to a syrupy consistency.

2 Remove from the heat and stir in the cream. Let cool and thicken. Store in a sealable jar in the refrigerator for up to 5 days.

coconut vanilla cream

Makes about ⅔ cup

Preparation time 5 minutes, plus chilling

1 (13½ oz) can coconut milk

1 teaspoon vanilla extract

1 tablespoon confectioners' sugar, sifted

Rich and indulgent, this whipped cream is a great replacement for thick heavy cream.

1 Place the can of coconut milk into the refrigerator for about 2 hours, until chilled.

2 Open the can and scoop out the thick coconut cream on the top, leaving the thin coconut water at the bottom (the coconut water can be stored in the refrigerator for about 3 days or frozen, for use in another recipe). Put about ⅔ cup of the thick coconut cream into a bowl.

3 Add the vanilla extract and confectioners' sugar and whip until smooth.

index

acknowledgments

Publisher's credits

Octopus Publishing Group would like to thank all the children featured in this book:
Quentin Deborne, De'shane Fringpone, Florence Kegg, Isabelle Kegg, Nelly Kegg, Celia
Leon, Timeo Leon, Finn May, Dora McHardy, Beatrice Offiler, Fañch Parker, and Miri Tobisawa.

Picture credits

Special photography by Ian Wallace.
Other photography:
Fotolia Tombaky 4 background (used throughout).
Octopus Publishing Group William Shaw 16.

Commissioning Editor: **Sarah Ford**
Senior Editor: **Leanne Bryan**
Art Director: **Tracy Killick at Tracy Killick Art Direction and Design**
Design Manager: **Jaz Bahra**
Photographer: **Ian Wallace**
Home economist and stylist: **Louise Pickford**
Picture Library Manager: **Jennifer Veall**
Assistant Production Manager: **John Casey**